# Bow Waves in the Bull Dust

a new edition of

# Leaves from the Peninsula

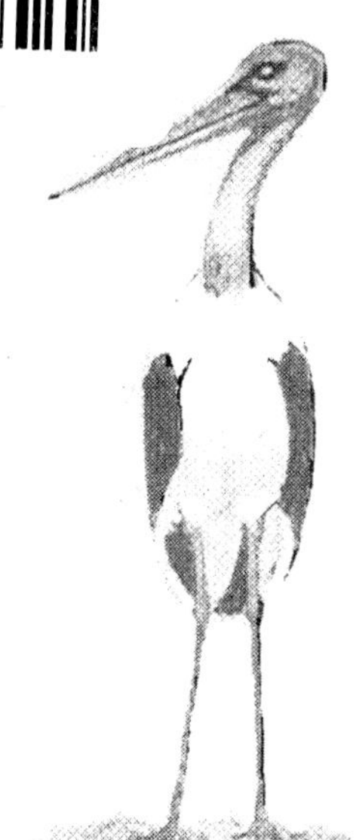

Lennie Wallace

First published in 1990 as *Leaves from the Peninsula*

Second published in 1999 by Central Queensland University Press

Third published in 2012 by Boolarong Press, Salisbury, Brisbane, Australia.

National Library of Australia Cataloguing-in-Publication entry

| | |
|---|---|
| Author: | Wallace, Lennie |
| Title: | Bow waves in the bull dust / Lennie Wallace. |
| ISBN: | 9781921920714 (pbk.) |
| Subjects: | Wallace, Lennie. |
| | Country life--Queensland--Cape York Peninsula. |
| | Ranch life--Queensland--Cape York Peninsula. |
| | Women ranchers--Queensland--Cape York Peninsula--Biography. |
| | Ranchers--Queensland--Cape York Peninsula--Biography. |
| Dewey Number: | 636.01092 |

The front cover painting is *Peninsula Back Blocks* by Len Cook

Printed and bound by Watson Ferguson and Company, Salisbury, Brisbane, Australia.

# CONTENTS

# INTRODUCTION

Cape York is a vast area. The portion within the Cook Shire alone is some 50,000 square miles in the way we used to measure land. That is, almost as large as all England. Yet in it, apart from the historic little town of Cooktown and the new company-owned town of Weipa, the white inhabitants are on Christian name terms with each other. They are friends and neighbours although they may live hundreds of miles apart and may see each other but once or twice a year at the Laura or Coen races.

They are united because they are so few, because they have a strong common bond of love for the Outback and because, perhaps, no one else is interested.

This story is between thirty and forty years old. It tells of a past era, albeit the recent past. The Peninsula has changed, and some would say, not for the better.

At the time of this true story, the Peninsula was a world of its own. Its cattle industry was still in the longhorn stage, and the entry of made roads and motor vehicles into the area, though welcome was met with a kind of distrust akin to that felt in the American Wild West when barbed wire was first introduced.

There are still no big company-owned stations in the Peninsula. The properties range from four and a half thousand square miles down to a handy two hundred square miles and are owned by individuals or families. Many of them are descendants of the miners who came to the Palmer goldfield in the 1870's, or of the teamsters, packers, and cattlemen who came with the prospectors.

Raising cattle in this area is still a family affair and most of the family trees have long since interlaced by growing so closely together. Some, like Ruth and Fred Shephard, and the elder Wallaces mentioned here, have since passed away.

A Government official called upon to furnish a report on the state of affairs in the Cook Shire reported 'an absolute lack of personal gain due to disadvantageous conditions, but an overwhelming presence of personal freedom.'

They are not a lethargic people. The men work from daylight till dark in a tropical climate, and so do most of the women. Nonetheless, there is a peace and freedom granted to those living in isolation that others more materially advanced may well envy. In this book, hardship was part of the life.

Lennie Wallace

MAP OF
CAPE YORK PENINSULA
Showing some of the places
mentioned in this book
0 10 25 50 100
SCALE IN MILES
TORRES STRAIT
THURSDAY ISLAND
Cape York
Pr of Wales Island
SOMERSET
Van Spult Head
BAMAGA
Jackey Jackey
Jardine R
McHenry R
Elliot R
Skardon R
McDONNELL
Shelburne Bay
Port Musgrave
Bertiehaugh
Bramwell
C Grenville
MAPOON
Temple Bay
Ducie R
Wenlock R
MORETON
ANDOOM
PORTLAND RDS
Restoration Id
Duyfken Pt
WEIPA
York Dns
Pascoe R
Merluna
IRON RANGE
GULF OF CARPENTARIA
Watson R
WENLOCK
Lockhart R
AURUKUN
Archer R
Great Barrier Reef
Nesbit R
Peach R
Rocky R
Cape Keerweer
Rokeby
Meripah
Blue Mt
Princess Charlotte Bay
Coen R
COEN
PORT STEWART
Flinders Ids
C Melville
Kendall R
Stewart R
Bathurst Bay
Holroyd R
EBAGOOLAH
Lilyvale
Edward R
Lukin R
Violet Vale
Morehead R
Lizard Id
Strathgordon
Kalpowar
Lakefield
EDWARD RIV
Strathmay
MUSGRAVE
Hann R
Kennedy R
Jack R
Starcke
C Flattery
Normanby R
C Bedford
Coleman R
Kalinga
Laura Stn
HOPE VALE
Koolburra
Olivevale
Alice R
Fairview
COOKTOWN
KOWANYAMA
Kimba
LAURA
Annan R
Koolatah
PALMERVILLE
Rutland Plns
LAKELAND
Helenvale
Dunbar
Palmer R
Butcher Hill
Bloomfield R
Nassau R
Byerstown Ra
C Tribulation
Mitchell R
Strathleven
MAYTOWN
Daintree R
Highbury
Mt Windsor
MOSSMAN
Mitchell R
MT CARBINE
Staaten R
PORT DOUGLAS
Hodgkinson R
Gamboola
MT MOLLOY
WALSH
Wrotham Pk
Barron R
THORNBORO
CAIRNS
Lynd R
Walsh R
MAREEBA
CHILLAGOE
GORDONVALE
ATHERTON
DIMBULAH
BABINDA
Tate R
Tableland
HERBERTON
INNISFAIL
G.PIKE
MT GARNET
RAVENSHOE

# 1.

# SMELL THE GUM LEAVES

We must have looked a motley crew as we stood on the tarmac waiting for the plane that was to take us back to Cooktown and the bush.

In our party there really were only Ruth, her father (the Boss) and myself but by a stroke of good luck, there were other bushies heading home as well.

Miles Morris, a next-door neighbour to Butcher Hill, was returning with a finger swathed in intricate bandaging, the result of an argument with another Morris—his truck. It had slipped back as he had tried to chock a wheel on a dangerous incline on the Byerstown Range pinning him very efficiently by the finger.

Perhaps if you disregarded the extremes of the other two, their four-inch sombreros and their high-heeled Williams boots, they might, in their town clothes, have passed for townies.

'Fat' was nattily turned out in high-heeled Santa Fe boots with sharp, square, stitched toes radiating a dazzling polish. Mick's number nines with high heels sloping a bit to the sides were much less dashing and were probably the same old elastic sides he had been wearing mustering, through thick and thin, through mud and manure, until his annual spree in the Big Smoke.

The six of us collectively stood out amongst the usual

inhabitants of suburbia. Ruth was still hobbling on crutches. She had broken her leg at the station six months earlier. She and the blackboy Paddy, had both jumped their horses out to block the one beast while drafting in the big receiving yard. Paddy's horse was a heavy clumper, a slightly fined-down draught-horse and Paddy's style of riding is rather fierce. There was a sharp crack as they collided a fraction from the bullock.

The crack came as the bone in Ruth's leg snapped under the impact. Her mare, frightened by the turn of events, began to pig-jump and it was many long agonising seconds before Ruth could be eased from the saddle.

Fortunately, the accident happened during the dry weather, that time of the year immediately after the wet monsoons, the time when all the station properties are busily engaged mustering, branding, spaying and selecting bullocks to put on the road to the saleyards. There was a road of sorts leading to Cooktown and after the properties using the road had spent several days working on it after the wet it was trafficable until the storms fell at the end of the year.

Ruth made the trip to town stretched stiffly on a mattress in the back of the station's only vehicle, a four ton Dodge truck, trying unsuccessfully to ignore the bumps and jolts.

Next morning, an ambulance plane had taken her carefully aboard at Cooktown and whisked her away to the nearest doctor — in Cairns. That had been six long weary months ago. During her six months' exile in the alien city she had celebrated her twenty-first birthday in the home of a kind but ageing aunt, well away from her mates and the loves of her life — her horses.

She had exchanged the life of the mustering camp and the joy of seeing the first foals born at the beginning of the storms for a routine of constant X-raying and renewals of plasters. The final plaster had been removed, the break pronounced healed and she was free to go home, back on the Boss's payroll and rearing to go. I was going to Butcher Hill on a similar mission.

Our income tax forms listed us as 'station hands' as did my marriage certificate a year or so later. For some obscure reason we scorned the term 'jillaroo' and thought of ourselves as 'ringers', the same as the men in the Northern mustering camps.

The surface of the runway was slippery and Ruth's crutches kept sliding despite helping hands from all sides. Fat and Micky were getting cold feet. Fat was all for getting a taxi back to town to put in another week of sipping iced refreshment. Mick was more than half-inclined to join him but this was to be Mick's first flight and curiosity triumphed.

As befitted the senior members of the party the Boss and Miles boarded the plane with more dignity than we did. Neither Ruth nor I liked air travel but this time it had its compensations. We were both going back to the bush after a much-too-long absence.

Mick kept up a commentary on the different landmarks as we flew over the coast. His favourite was Mount Peter Botte. According to Mick we flew over it four times.

When he was about to claim yet another peak as his fifth Peter Botte a man across the aisle could stand it no longer.

"Pardon", he said, "That is Gold Hill. We have yet to come to Peter Botte."

That silenced Mick for a while but he was soon in his stride naming the rivers as they entered the sea.

Cooktown itself may not have much to offer in the way of breath-taking beauty, but all the same, Captain Cook's anchorage and the small town do make a very inviting picture as the aircraft circles preparatory to landing.

The township nestles against a hillside on one edge of the estuary and tapers off to a wooded point from which the red of the blossoming poinciana flames out from the green of the native foliage.

On the opposite side of the river is a line of strangely shaped mountains, one called most aptly, Mount Fantastic. These hills have all the colour of a tropical green butterfly's wing in the sunshine and the beauty of opal in the glowing sunset when the dying sun coaxes brilliant gem tints from the silver of the harbour.

In short, it was good to be back. But home was still more than fifty rough miles away.

We said good-bye to our fellow travellers at the Airways Office and proceeded to a friend's home to change to riding clothes. Not that it was necessary to ride out at this time of the year but the road was rough and very dusty and riding in the back of the truck as we would be, shirts and trousers were the order of the day.

Ruth's clothes were the same she had worn when Paddy's horse had collided with her. Her small riding boots, one with the careful stitching trying to hide where it had been cut from her swollen foot, her old pocket knife and half-empty match tin, were dusted and waiting.

Until 1950, the trip from town had meant a day spent in riding or driving to Helenvale and then another long day's ride to Butcher Hill. This time (April, 1950) we had left Cairns early in the morning and had reached home the same day. Little short of miraculous.

Disappointment awaited us when we did reach the station. The plant had gone out without us. Meanwhile we were house-bound. Ruth hobbled about on crutches and I in the way of one who walks with a limping friend hobbled around after her.

We were repairing gear, very simple stuff like making straps, hammering rivets into broken bits of leatherwork and the masterpiece, making ourselves a new saddle-bag each.

We carried our 'needlework' wherever we went rolling wax ends and adding stitches from time to time. We took them to the yards as we measured water to be added to the cattle dip, a very difficult job requiring great physical and mental effort! We had to turn a tap and fill a five hundred gallon tank. That done we had to turn on another tap which allowed the measured water to flow into the dip. If the dip was very low we might even have to repeat the performance and put two tankfuls in.

While waiting for the tank to fill we stitched, for it would never do to neglect the running water and to run the risk of wasting a very precious commodity. It was quite pleasant sitting in the shade of the tank on the cool couch grass, sewing and talking. As Paddy didn't kill the two death adders from the grass under the tank until a few days later, ignorance was bliss!

The saddle-bags took such a long time to make. Although the initial stitching was very neat and small the final dash was inclined to the 'homeward bound' style. We were neck-and-neck at the finish. Needles were thrust back through the last few awl holes to end off. Knots were hurriedly tied and we raced to the kitchen to show Ruth's mother the finished products!

When the excitement died down Ruth looked around for her crutches. They were nowhere to be seen. In the race to be first to the kitchen broken legs were forgotten and the crutches were left propped against the bench in the gear room. Ruth left them there, stacked in one corner until we were able to return them to the hospital in Cairns.

Before leaving her crutch days behind, Ruth went for a few rides from the house. There were two old horses left by the plant for homestead use, the old night-horse Ginger and an equally senile mare, Ginger's Mate. At any other time we would have scorned being seen on such a pair of nondescripts but after our exile both Ginger and his mate looked in Melbourne Cup class to us.

For a start Ginger looked somewhat askance at the strange creature with an extra pair of legs that approached him and at times he even managed a skittish shy and a skip away but he soon became used both to Ruth and to the way she had to mount.

Her broken leg was the one that normally takes the weight in getting on a horse. In its present stage it wasn't nearly strong enough to boost her up and into the saddle. She would manoeuvre her foot into the stirrup and look about hopefully for assistance. This was when I was supposed to hoist her up and into the saddle/seat.

Unfortunately Ruth was unusually ticklish and the moment I'd touch her she'd collapse giggling. It was infectious and we would have to begin again and again.

Bill who was the strong silent type didn't hold with giggling females or anything that menaced the smooth running of his plant. He'd step in and swing Ruth up with one manly heave. One time he overdid the muscle and Ruth just saved herself from going right overboard by the skin of her teeth. The surprised look on her face as she sailed gaily into space was reason enough without considering the all-over effect, but neither of us was game to laugh. Bill had us more than a little bit bluffed.

When the company was lacking in strong male arms Ruth was loath to dismount for any reason. I can't say I encouraged her either. One day while mustering horses Ruth had talked her mother into coming out for a last ride and the three of us were holding a mob of horses while the men scouted around for a few that were missing. Ruth's mare, Sally, began to change her weight from leg to leg with the strain of the long wait. Then, suddenly (we hadn't taken the leg-changing as warning) she lay down. Ruth was helpless. She just sat. Like a kid playing at cowboys with a saddle over a fallen log. She was absolutely helpless.

With a grunt Sally threatened to roll right over!

"Quick!" cried Ruth. "Someone! Do something!"

We flew off our horses and raced to her rescue. Sally just lay there while Ruth extricated her foot from under the old dear's ribs who made no attempt to rise until a well-placed boot-toe gave her a nudge.

Time dragged heavily waiting for the camp to come in. I had never met Ruth's brother Bill who was supposed to be very shy — of women in particular. On previous stays at Butcher Hill I would either have missed Bill by a day or two or else he was due the day after I had to leave. This was probably very much to his liking but I don't think he deliberately planned it. The year before it was a cyclone and subsequent flooding delayed him and his cattle and though I think he is pretty smart I don't really believe he could whip up a cyclone just to postpone our meeting!

It was a happy morning when we looked up towards the yards and saw the plant horses coming down through the top paddock. Ruth and I were a trifle miffed that Bill hadn't waited those extra couple of days so that we could have gone out too so we decided we wouldn't exactly rush out and fall prostrate with joy when Bill Wallace and Edwin Gostelow did make an appearance.

We needn't have wasted out time cultivating that sufficiently disinterested look. Bill didn't turn up with the rest. He was burning grass. And when he did turn up we didn't see him ride in. In fact, with the wiry whiskers that graced his face and a good inch about it, it was difficult to see him at all.

He muttered "Pleased to meet you." Shook my hand and had his dinner (lunch) at four o'clock.

After a few unsuccessful attempts by us to start conversation we retreated to wash-up the dishes and Bill slipped away, thankfully, I think, to see to the few head of straggler cattle he had picked up and brought home.

It wasn't a very romantic meeting but the upshot was that three weeks later Bill decided we'd get married. I was all in agreement but it was six months before we managed it.

The main stumbling block was that I was under twenty-one at the time and that meant Bill had to write to my mother first to "get a receipt" for me (his phrase). He certainly hated writing letters! Ruth and I tried all ways to get hold of the one he eventually wrote but he wouldn't hand it over for inspection.

Neither would my mother.

# 2.

# FATS FOR THE ROAD

The plant had barely arrived home than it was time to go out again. Clothes were washed. Cooked and uncooked food was stowed in packbags. Loose horseshoes were attended to and swags were rolled and strapped down across the loaded packbags as top loads. This time our swags were with the others.

Bill and I were out scouting together, the idea being that should we find cattle, I would hold them while he found more. We could then drive the combined effort into the mob sure that the area was left clear of stock.

I was riding a mare named Music. She was a delight to ride — free in her action and with a springy walk but — and there's always a 'but' with horses — take her out for a walk in timbered country and she was a horror. Plenty of horses hit trees but Music deliberately aimed at them and, like Annie Oakley she never missed.

We were mustering a corner of the run where lost droving cattle were sometimes found. A natural barrier of steep hills prevented them from going back to their old home run and they were trapped. As they were usually mean old rogues who had eluded the nightwatch or sneaked off under cover of bushes in broad daylight, they were very difficult to find.

Some had been old bags of bones left to die by long-suffering drovers but they had recovered on the sweet basalt grasses and when they did they reverted to the galloping tactics of the wily scrub pikers they had once been. Drovers' cattle were something that could guarantee a lively ride.

It was a band of these ruffians that caused my fall from grace. For once in my life I saw the cattle before Bill. A roan cow with her head peeking over the lip of the gully was the first sighted. The others were almost out of sight in the gully itself. I did think we were riding a bit too close to them but it didn't cross my mind that Bill hadn't spotted them.

They heard us and took off, the roan cow in the lead, racing for the hills. Bill was right behind them and gaining. Music and I were a bad last.

After the first few hundred yards, my knees were reduced to pulp by Music's bulldozing action on sapling and tree alike. The more I tried to pull her off them, the more determined she became. I tried to give her a free rein but that wasn't what she wanted either. When Bill did block the cattle and they turned around to face us I heaved a sigh of relief and sagged in the middle.

I should have known better. It was just a tactical pause. The next two seconds were something like a Mandrake comic strip. One second, Bill and the cattle were there — the next split second they had vanished. Although I hadn't the slighest idea which way they had gone I set out in pursuit.

"I'll track them," I promised trying to redeem myself but forgetting in my eagerness to trace their tracks from where I had last seen them. I would turn up just at the crucial moment in a strategic position, save the day and make amends for my idiocy.

So much for flights of fancy. Bill tracked me up about an hour later looking not at all pleased with me or the situation.

"Why didn't you stop where you were if you couldn't keep up?"

The "if you couldn't keep up" bit sounded unfair, but having no logical reply to make I meekly bowed my head and followed him in silence and at what I hoped was a respectful distance back to the mob.

The cattle had split in six different directions and beaten him on a steep pinch. It would have been handy to have someone there to back him up he commented, as he told the tale that night in the camp but we sighted them again the next day (miraculously) and this time Secret and I ran them until they pulled up. We delivered five to the mob. The sixth, a great gaunt roan piker, wild of eye and a bit too free with his spikey horns, kept charging me when I tried to hunt him up into the mob Bill was steadying in the lead. Bill finally threw him and slit his throat.

We were mustering fats for the road. It didn't take long. The whole run could be mustered in about five weeks of continuous going. At the same time we branded calves, spayed any cull females, dehorned weaners and dipped the entire bovine population to keep tick and buffalo fly at bay.

Bullock muster is one of the best times of the year. For a short few months the grass is of a dazzling greenness. The rivers and swamps are full, yet serene. The time of boggy sandridges and the muddy turbulence of flood waters is past and the heat and misery of the "Dry" has yet to come. Our horses were sleek and fat, ready and willing to gallop to block any beast that didn't want to co-operate.

Life was good and our small world a happy place.

Daily the number of bullocks grew. At some camps there was a paddock for them. At other times they had to be "tailed-out" on grass and water while more were mustered. Ruth, Leo and I usually shared this boring chore with Edwin or Paddy.

They were all yarded at night.

Birds were everywhere. We saddled up and rode away from the camp to the accompaniment of the magpies' song. We mustered to the whirring of cicadas punctuated by the raucous voices of parrots feeding on the blossom and seed; nightly the men checked their watches by a kookaburra chorus as we lay on our swags around the fire talking until sleep overtook us.

Each evening the more melodious bush noises were obliterated by the bawling of the calves as the hot brands singed their hides and the knife and ear-pliers drew blood. Once let back with their mothers a good long drink of milk and a few reassuring licks from their mums seemed to effect a hundred per cent recovery.

Butcher Hill was a small run of three hundred and fifty square miles. Big "clean skins" were a rarity so there was no need for a broncho horse to pull the unbranded stock up to a broncho frame for branding as was the rule on many places further out. Calves were mostly scruffed with someone holding the head and another the hind legs while branding was done. Paddy was very quick at catching calves and flipping them over on to the ground so that the operation was over in a flash. Through the rails of the adjoining yard mothers thrust their noses and lowed encouragement, concern and motherly love.

From camp to camp we moved, driving the fat lazy bullocks with us. They moved along leisurely, their snow white faces deep in the bright green grass as they fed along; their ruby-red hides gleamed in the sunlight.

At that time Butcher Hill ran Hereford cattle although there were some with a dash of Zebu brought in by Glen Prairie bulls descended from the Zebus imported from the United States in 1933. The imported cattle looked strange with their huge humps and the Boss wrote a letter or two to the cattlemen's news weekly complaining of their import. Once he saw the results of the cross-breeding he changed sides and was the author of many more Letters to the Editor supporting them. However he didn't like to be reminded of his first impressions!

While mustering, the horses went ahead of us to a new camp. When we arrived just on dusk with the cattle we would come to a rigged camp with smoke rising in a blue spiral from the fire, with bells clanging on the grazing plant-horses, with packsaddles ranged neatly on a sapling saddle-rack and best of all with the appetising smell of hot crusty damper, simmering stew and steaming tea.

From time to time we went back to the homestead to paddock our bullocks and to renew our tucker supply but on one muster we stayed out longer than planned and the tucker-bags were empty.

Bill decided he'd put in a few extra days at this camp and Ruth and I, with old Maureen the tucker-horse, were sent home for more flour, tea and jam.

All was going beautifully, Maureen alternately jogging along or stopping to feed ahead of us, until we saw something that made Ruth and I seek each other's confirmation. We couldn't believe our eyes. Nor could Maureen. She began to shy and cavort in a totally unbecoming way to one so big and heavy, and snort loudly.

A mysterious something had flattened a wide strip in the lightly timbered forest, rooting out great trees and laying them in untidy rows on either side of the cleared swathe.

It finished as abruptly as it began only a few hundred yards ahead of us. The devastation was rather frightening. Our horses thought so too, and began pussy-footing along, shying, snorting and almost shooting out from under us.

We didn't think of the obvious answer until we saw the tracks of the bulldozer. Our thoughts had run more to the hurricanes we had heard about at school. Hurricanes could cut narrow swathes in jungles, forests, cities and native villages alike and the back of our necks prickled at the thought of our possible doom, death and certain annihilation.

The bulldozer was merely making a new road. One that was to go to Laura. Our knowledge of news was what each ringer reported around the fire at night or what we read in our months-old dinner wrapping-paper. If cities were bombed and governments changed it was done without our knowledge.

The existing road, the road to Mareeba, branched off from the Laura route near Butcher Hill. The Laura "road" was a very humble bush track made for horsemen. It contented itself with going around trees rather than knocking them down and removing them.

The cleared strip ended as abruptly as it had begun. The contractor was only given a contract for a mile of clearing. This mile probably contained the heaviest basalt and the biggest trees and with no road either behind or before him over which he could travel, his problems with the ever present breakages were astronomic. To get a part for his 'dozer he would have to wend his slow way in to tiny Cooktown, order what was necessary and wait a week until the weekly launch came with what he hoped was the correct item. But there it was, the huge basalt boulders his monument forever — a lovely cleared mile of devastation in the middle of nowhere.

Gradually, the Main Roads added bits to the original section until the road snaked through the Laura River valley to the township of Laura, but we found the sudden swift change from virgin forest to "road" rather breath-taking.

We could have taken the long safe way and gone around the hurricane's swathe but being an exclusively female touring party curiosity triumphed.

Our two saddle horses were part-bred Arabs and this particular strain had a tendency to shy at nothing and to duck their heads and pig-jump at any excuse at all. Whatever they did they did it with the utmost zing, zoom and zest so that our progress was a zigzag as they shied from one side of the fallen timber to the other.

It was a bit eerie but the two saddle horses seemed to see possibilities of an endless supply of ferocious lions, tigers and tyrannosauri lurking in the uprooted trees. Even the usually staid Maureen became infected by their demeanour shying and snorting with them.

Bits of broken branch hung precariously in the limbs of trees still standing and when the wind sprang up a couple of these fell down, one just in front of us and the other noisily but neatly behind. Fortunately we were both sitting tight in our saddles and survived our mount's attempts to be both free of us and to flee. If it had been otherwise the rest of the camp would have starved until someone sallied forth to find our mangled remains — or more importantly — the tucker.

When we did reach the men and the bulldozer we were forced

to exchange greetings with loud yells from a safe distance for while our trusty steeds would not take one step further towards that terrible monster, neither could the trusty steeds be trusted to stay tied to trees while we paid social calls.

The first few years of roads nearly drove the horses mad with the accompanying traffic. The cattle couldn't have cared less what juggernauts came hurtling along excepting the few that were shot for beef or were knocked down by motorists.

The newly-cleared road held a great fascination for all the animals — except the horses. The cattle gloried in the soft dustiness and no manner of honking, banging or yelling could shift them from their chosen beds when once they had settled for the night. The easiest thing to do was to go around them.

Edwin loved tracks. The roads supplied dozens of them and under Edwin's tutelage we soon became reasonably adept in recognising them. Snake and goanna tracks were old stuff. Wallabies, too. The road opened up to us the tinier world of dainty native cat pads, 'possum tracks where they had scuttled down one tree, hurried across the road and scurried up a tree on the other side. Sometimes if we were early enough we could see one race back up the tree trunk for safety and could see the shine of two little black eyes peering from a hollow limb. Dingo pads were commonplace. They'd follow along after travellers whether they were in trucks, on horseback or with cattle. Wild pigs were so numerous their tracks weren't worth a second glance.

Birds were there in all sizes from the tiniest little wrens to the emu with his feathery bustle that bobbed up and down as he ran from us often with a clutch of striped chicks. Butcher birds and bower birds frequented most of the camps. Like wagtails they seemed to seek human company and showed absolutely no fear. The black and white butcher birds had to be watched. They would swoop into the tent and steal anything they thought might be edible if it were left unprotected.

I always searched bower birds' playgrounds in the hope of finding a nugget of at least gold-bearing quartz but the closest I came to finding a fortune was when I found a two shilling coin in a bower just off the drovers' road at old Northedge.

When we arrived back at the homestead with all the bullocks the drover was already there. He was to take the station plant and one of the station stockboys while he provided a couple of extra droving hands from the Mareeba side.

The trip over the Byerstown Range to Mareeba would take them seventeen to eighteen days. A real "picnic" one of the "boys" assured us with plenty of grass and water. The saleyards at Mareeba had been in existence for a few years and were a great boon to the Northern cattlemen. Before the saleyards offered buyer competition the vendor was at the buyer's mercy. He either took the price offered — or walked the cattle back again. And the latter course had been taken on occasions when the price offered was ridiculously low.

Bill and Edwin were to go with the drovers for a couple of nights so that the cattle could be double-watched at night while they were close to their home run. Once along the road the cattle would settle down and our two men would no longer be required.

All hands turned out to give the cattle a start away. Ruth and I rode along on the tail feeling rather gleeful that some old rogue was going and feeling rather sad that there were two quiet old milkers' bullocks setting off to their fate as well.

We said goodbye to the drovers at their dinner camp on the river and, in the absence of the Boss, cantered most of the way home, Ruth making her little mare, Mona, rear up to put her fore-hoofs on high antbeds for good measure. It was a habit that she later gave away when her horse's front legs sank down through a hollow antbed and we had to expend considerable time and energy getting it free.

The bullocks were gone and we had two days "off" coming to us.

# 3.

# KNOCK DOWN THE BREAD

We were more than ready to sit back and enjoy our two days off when Ruth's mother dropped her bombshell. It shattered our peace of mind and ruined our sleep for months to come.

It wasn't that she said much. As a bit of an aside as we said 'Good-night' hoping for an early night, she said, "I leave on Saturday."

It was Thursday night. We were dumbfounded.

Of course, we knew that she was going but in the excitement of the muster we had no time to think of matters as mundane as house-keeping. Anyway, we didn't think she'd go.

The Boss had bought a farm on the Tablelands, a dairying and fattening property and Ruth's mother was to live there.

We were to be station cooks!

Ruth had learnt the art at school and I had an Honours Pass in Invalid Cookery. That entailed little more than poaching eggs, slicing up repulsively gooey eggwhites for Albumin Water and making doubtful eggflips. Hardly a repertoire for working men or women.

In any case, there were no eggs. Once we took to the bush with the plant, the hens took to the bush also. Many's the mile I've trudged through long grass, taipans, bindies and bushes just because some fool hen sung out and a bigger fool human thought it meant 'egg'.

For all our previous experience we weren't fit cooks for the job. It was no comfort, either, that we were aware of our short-comings. The last hours — our two days off — were spent poring over stacks of recipes in book form and on torn-out pages from women's magazines.

Adding to our misery the Boss was on a diet. We would scrounge most painstakingly for eggs to cook him what he should have eaten, only to see him help himself to what he shouldn't have eaten. No one could blame him. Eggs are monotonous. But it was hard on the nerves — his as well as ours and we paid doubly for his non-adherence to diet.

Breadmaking was to be one of our chores. We had stood beside Ruth's mother countless times as she mixed dough, knocked it back or put it into tins but our minds were never on what she was doing. We were always busily telling her of our doings in the limited orbit of the mustering camp so, on that fateful Friday night, she took us on a tour of the store room to show us what was what.

"Your father can't eat this. It doesn't agree with him. Bill and Edwin like fruit cake. Plenty of mixed fruit up there away from the ants. The recipe's in the C.W.A. book."

"Cook plenty of rice for the boys. Use it when the potatoes run out, too. Baked green bananas make a good substitute for potatoes in the Wet, too.

"Those seeds I planted should be up soon and ready to plant out. If you look after them you'll have fresh veges for a while."

Our worried faces showed the strain of the mental gymnastics as we tried to work out a schedule involving cooking, laundry work, house work, gardening, milking, feeding the two pet foals and trying to keep the Boss satisfied with our work in the camp at the same time.

It became torture to listen to Ruth's mother's voice as it droned on punctuated occasionally by wails of:

"How did you say to make white sauce?"

"How much soda and cream of tartar to a cup of flour?"

"How do you know if it's cooked?"

The last question rather forlorn and lacking confidence.

Then it was decided that, although there was a great quantity of bread baked in reserve, I should try my hand under "supervision". Ruth's mother supervised for a start and sent me for a dipper of warm water to add with the yeast to the hollowed-out mound of flour and salt she had sifted into the bread dish.

She removed the cork from the yeast bottle with one deft movement and let it squirt its milky contents into the flour.

"Now, mix it," she said as she and Ruth prepared to continue their tour down the line of shelves.

She didn't think to tell me to get a spoon or fork and I had seen her doing something to the bread with her hands, so I washed my hands, literally bogged in and 'mixed it'.

The more I tried the worse it got. The dough stuck to everything.

My nose became itchy. I couldn't scratch. My hair fell into my eyes. I was helpless. Then a flying ant headed for my ear. That was more than I could stand. Dough and all, I swatted him. I adjusted my hair, rubbed my nose which had stopped itching when I attacked the insect and called for help.

"Add more flour" advised the experienced bread-baker from the dim distance of the end of the shelves.

I did. It was still sticky.

"Add some more."

I did and kept adding until it was no longer gluey but just a sodden, fairly round, lump. Then, having been the length of the shelves my "supervisor" returned.

"Heavens! That's miles too much flour! I only use half that. Never mind. You can't do anything about it now. Just remember time, tide and bread wait for no man. It'll be ready to knock back at daylight."

Next morning we bade a tearful farewell to the travellers and were sauntering back to wake the chooks when I remembered — Bread! Gee! It'd be over-risen and flowing from its dish to meet me at the door.

I ran in and threw back the cover. It lay there, a sodden lump, possibly two and a half sizes larger than it had been the night before. I stood hesistantly until a voice from the door announced confidently:

"You knock it back now." Ruth had arrived.

"How?"

"You know. Like Mum did."

I had been at her elbow while she made bread but I couldn't recall what she had done. I gave it a good pummelling and pounding until it reduced its bulk slightly and my arms signalled it was time to desist.

I remembered to put the covers back over the dough. Dough, contrary to its appearance, is delicate stuff and must be protected against chills. Quite often my dough suffered the agonies of double pneumonia, pleurisy and complications.

The knocking-back done, the dough had to be left to rise again. Whereupon it was to be pounced upon once more, knocked back again, formed into loaves and left in greased tins to "double its bulk". That done it was to be cooked in a very hot oven for one hour.

I knew this last bit and stoked up a beautiful fire for the job. Could he have seen it, Old Nick would have hired me as head fireman for eternity.

I wanted to put the loaves in the oven with a professional flourish and walk nonchalantly away looking confident that the batch would turn out featherlight, crisp and crusty. But there was no one to watch and I was more than doubtful about the bread even being edible so I slid the loaves into the oven, carefully closed the door on them and slunk away to wait.

Three-quarters of an hour later, during which time I had paced back and forth in front of the oven trying not to look like an expectant father, Ruth called from the doorway,

"How's the bread?"

I frowned at the sudden loudness of her voice. Why, a shock like that might cause the dough to sink to the bottom of the tins!

"I don't know," I whispered. "It's only been in for three-quarters of an hour."

"Didn't you look? You're supposed to turn it, you know."

"Oooh," I didn't know. I thought bread was like sponge cakes and dropped in the middle if you opened the door prematurely.

Patiently Ruth advised me to check.

With several layers of insulating material I opened the door. The smoke sent me reeling back until the kitchen table blocked my retreat.

As the smoke cleared I advanced again. The bread was certainly cooked! It also had a nice hump rising from the middle of its back. At least it hadn't collapsed in the middle. Besides, it was much better to have overcooked bread than undercooked — wasn't it?

The next shock came as I lifted the loaves to the top of the safe to cool. Some strength I may have but I lack weightlifter's muscle.

A truck noise shattered the calm after the storm. Visitors! We raced around ineffectually wondering what to do. The bread couldn't be hidden. It was still too warm to put away.

The callers were a couple of Main Roads men engaged in building the road optimistically called the Mulligan 'Highway'.

We sat them down to tea and cake, only making the minor mistake of serving boiled custard instead of milk. Archie, the more senior of the two, advised us of our mistake. The younger fellow, more polite, drank his tea with custard and said nothing.

They had passed the Butcher Hill truck along the road. All was going well, no troubles. They'd had dinner together at the Kelly's and parted company. Oh, a limb did smash the top of the piano, but what was one piano more or less?

Our shocked silence encouraged them to enlarge on the damage until we finally woke up our legs were being pulled — and pulled hard.

As we were entertaining our guests in the kitchen, they

couldn't help seeing the bread cooling on the safe-top. I very modestly told the tale of its making, telling what a failure it was, stressing all its bad points in the hope someone would contradict. As I had used double the usual amount of flour, it certainly looked all right from a distance. Finally Archie rose to inspect it.

"There's nothing wrong with that," he pronounced after lengthy scrutiny with his one good eye. "That's good bread."

A breathless hush as he picked it up. His arm dropped swiftly to his side, the bread nearly continued on to the floor. Archie carefully replaced it on the safe with a grim two-handed hold and said:

"Oh, well, we all make mistakes."

And whether he referred to my bread or to his previous statement I guess it all boiled down to the same thing.

We cooked week about with the outgoing cook using the kitchen on Saturday morning and the incoming cook using it that afternoon. In theory that ensured leisure for all on Sunday — if we were home.

Of course, the work of the mustering plant still had to go on. Ruth looked after the house and laundry while I had the garden and chooks to balance up. In the Dry, Ruth also added to her issue the feeding of the animals, the stallion and numerous brood mares with or without foals. When the Dry was really upon us and cattle work had degenerated to showing cattle water soaks and spraying weak cows in outside yards to kill the ticks that fed on their blood, Ruth stayed home to devote her energies to the house and to the animals on supplementary rations.

Although we were told repeatedly that bread was to wait for no man, ours was often forced to wait for us.

The cook was allowed to leave the cattle before we reached the house-paddocks in order to get tea ready and to attend to the bread's whims. Sometimes it had over-risen, overflowed to the floor and was on the way to the door to greet us when we arrived. At other times it looked little different when we got home to what it had been when we left.

The yeast bottle was a horror. It was supposed to be re-made regularly to keep it sweet and to ensure the yeast lived. Our days away from home didn't help. And to make a batch of bread we had first to make fresh yeast which took at least twelve hours to become active.

Ruth put her thumb out of joint once when the cork flew out with more than its usual vigour. Edwin pulled the thumb back into gear but the cork was lost. I don't know how many corks we did lose. Interplanetary missiles had nothing on them. They would sail magnificently up through the rafters of the unceiled storeroom to land on the ceiling of the adjacent dining room. Corks were soon at a premium.

Bill and Edwin were called in to stand by and remove corks while we set the bread. Finally, watching me flounder about in the sticky mess, Bill shouldered me out of the way with a "You're like an old cow in a bog!" and showed us how to do it.

Our bread did improve a little after that but we did have minor upsets. Someone left the door open and the old cat camped on the dough leaving a tell-tale trail of hair on the tea-towel and a very flat piece of dough beneath it. And another anonymous soul left a window open so that the cook returned to find bread dish and cover but no dough.

As we were often camped out for a week to a fortnight, the yeast bottle soon went to rack and ruin. We took advice from everyone and tried to "hot her up" with all manner of experiments from lemon juice to potato water, rice water and sultanas. No wonder the general opinion was that our bread was "crook". The day of dry or compressed yeast had not dawned and our routine didn't allow for regular yeast bottle treatment. We did try to take the bottle out in the camp with us but after a couple of corks blew out in a pack bag we gave up.

Whereas horse magazines and westerns had once been our regular reading material we now read cookery books to the exclusion of all else.

We used the names in the index as a guide, passing over the good old standby of a Victoria Sandwich because, as Edwin pointed out, this was North Queensland.

A Fail Me Never Cake was Ruth's masterpiece. It Failed Me Ever so I gave up after the fifth attempt.

A prime favourite was a chocolate cake that required no eggs and which had won some lucky lady a hundred pounds ($200) in a recipe contest. It was worth a thousand to us with the hens often on strike.

We made the recipe up as an eggless chocolate cake until the cocoa ran out. Then we served it as Eggless Coffee and Eggless Milo until both coffee and Milo ran out. For a while it was just eggless cake dolled up with a little icing and coconut until Ruth unearthed an old tin of malted milk. We baked an Eggless Malted Milk Cake, possibly the only one on record. I don't recommend it. It would certainly never have won a prize, even a five shillings (50c) one!

# 4.

# EAT UP YOUR GREEN ANTS

When Ruth's mother left the homestead a sixth member joined the mustering camp. She was Leo, the Aboriginal house girl.

Leo was really named "Leah" but apparently "Leo" is easier to the native tongue and "Leo" she was until she died. Similarly "Cecily" who later helped me with the children was called "Cecil".

Leo with her husband Paddy were the only natives then employed on Butcher Hill. They were both wards of the Protector (the Cooktown police) and were signed on each year at the Police Station. The bulk of Paddy's wages were paid direct to the Protector and placed to his credit.

From this fund, by our calculations then over the thousand pounds ($2,000) mark, Paddy received his "orders" of clothes and necessities each year. For special events such as the race meetings (the annual gathering of the tribes) he would receive extra pocket money and money for special purchases such as a wind-up gramophone and old 78 records or a radio.

Each week the Boss paid Paddy pocket money and an allowance of tobacco. The latter was plug tobacco in a solid cake from which tobacco was shaved off with a pocket knife as required. It was very strong and occasionally Leo would chew hers as an alternative to her ever-present pipe.

Paddy had been bred on the station coming there as a child with a brother and a sister. He took the family's name as his surname — Paddy Wallace — but was also known as Paddy Butcher Hill in the district.

Emily, Paddy's sister, was trained as a domestic in a Cooktown hotel but was an excellent stockman and returned to the bush and the mustering camp after she married. She was also a top camp cook and her Johnny Cakes made of dough and cooked slowly on coals were delicious. Golden brown and without one speck of coal embedded they must have been what the originator of the recipe had in mind when he invented it.

Peter, the third member of the family, died and was buried at the station.

Having spent his childhood with the other Wallace children Paddy had lost many of the old tribal beliefs but Leo was a "proper myall". She was a firm believer in Quinken, the Aboriginal ghosts that are surprisingly white, and all the tribal remedies and, to us, superstitions.

Think of the thinnest person you know and divide her by two. The result halved again would be Leo and as black is a colour recommended to matrons wishing to appear slimmer than they are, Leo looked even skinnier than perhaps she was.

After years in the mustering camp Leo became sick and died of the effects of a heart abnormally enlarged. Her grass-stem legs swelled to twenty times their usual diameter which made her think someone had put a curse on them. While Paddy was camped-out she and the old yard-boy Micky Bluetongue, would sit by a small fire until almost daylight to be sure no more evil spirits would creep in to their quarters. Naturally these sleepless nights did nothing to help her condition.

Part of the cure was to resist the evil spirits so Leo insisted she was "alri" and tried to continue with her work. When she did agree to go in to town to see the Matron she and Paddy rode in. By this time Leo was having dizzy spells and as they rode across one creek Leo blacked out and fell from her horse. The water revived her and her reflexes were still quick enough to grab the tail of

Paddy's horse as she was washed downstream.

Norman the mailman gave them a ride in to town from Helenvale and the Matron quickly despatched Leo to Cairns Base Hospital by Aerial Ambulance.

Micky had been treating Leo with green ants, the universal painkiller amongst the blacks. Micky's half-sister (same father, different mother) Annie recommended quinine bark.

Annie and Micky were a generation older than Paddy and Leo and had been brought up in tribal ways. In those days a man had several wives who were often sisters. They came from the Battle Camp area and Annie carried on her back scars from a hunting incident as a child.

While hunting, a big goanna being chased, ran up the small Annie's bare back. The claw marks became infected and must have been extremely painful. The infection then spread to an eye and Annie lost her sight in that eye giving her the name of Annie One Eye. She was a happy soul so it couldn't have left too many scars on her psyche.

Leo wasn't very confident in green ants and quinine; she preferred stewed sandalwood bark. According to Mick this was her undoing.

"I bin tell 'im. I bin tell 'im two t'ousand time. More better 'e eat green ant."

Before Leo came out with the musterers she had done very little riding. An occasional jaunt for the cows when they were too far away to be driven home on foot was the extent of her equestrienne experience. She soon learned — the hard way.

At first Bill was not too happy about the new member of his plant. It was no rarity for Aboriginal stockman's wives to take their place in the stock camps in the Peninsula — Emily was eagerly sought after as a top hand — but Bill thought three females in a camp of six was a bit too much for any self-respecting ringer.

That was probably why he left her, on her first day out, to wait on the road for Paddy. Paddy, as usual, was away for hours and when he did return he was given a hot reception.

A loyal Aboriginal family at Butcher Hill (now Lakeland) in the 'fifties – Doughboy, a dignified old gentleman, his wife Annie, and son Ernie.

Peninsula drovers set out on the long ride north behind the packhorse plant after delivering cattle at Mareeba, 1958.

The Laura-Coen road a few years ago.

Unknowingly Ruth and I were the cause of it We had given Paddy and Leo a horsey magazine to look at. One of the stories was about a big rough-looking horse not unlike Leo's "Sago". But the horse in the story was a "devil of a horse" and there was a drawing of him to prove it. Bucking frantically, eyes rolling, hoofs striking, tangled mane flying and at his rear end, instead of the usual equine bit of bone, beef and horsehair, he sported a forked "devil's tail".

Waiting alone for Paddy, Leo became convinced Sago had sprouted a Quinken tail too and for hours she sat motionless, perishing for a drink of water from the spring beside her but not game even to turn her head towards that forked tail in case the Quinken put a spell on her.

A big joke to us but not to Leo.

Leo soon settled into the ways of the camp and became a very useful member. She developed a liking for shirts with bullock horns on the pockets, stars on her hatband and fancy gear in general.

She was very envious of a bridle Ruth had of plaited strands of red, white and blue silk decorated with horseshoe-shaped buckles. Eventually it changed hands for a cash down-payment and the balance paid in services rendered. After that, stars appeared on it in new and glorious galaxies in a direct proportion to the way they disappeared from an old leather breastplate of Ruth's in the cobwebs of the saddle shed. They ceased to appear only when the breastplate became totally denuded of its Milky Way.

Leo had a close call when she was bringing up the station milkers one evening on foot. A large brown snake bit her twice on her bare ankle.

By the time she got to the house where the Boss quickly treated it the old way by incising the bite and tying a ligature above it, the blood had taken on a dark brown colour and had congealed. The Boss had to use the flattened blade of his pocket knife to scrape down Leo's leg to get the blood to ooze (not flow) from the wound. The odd drop that fell permanently stained the white Leichhardt wood floor boards on the verandah despite Leo's later attempts to scrub them away.

Some months previously a doctor had ridden through with a party studying 'possums and the possibility of the spread of virus diseases through 'possums. While he was staying at the homestead, Boxer, the old cattle dog, caught a snake and was bitten.

He recovered and the doctor told us he was probably immune and that if a young dog was bitten it might be worth a try to inoculate it with some of Boxer's blood to see if the antibodies in it would be effective. When he reached home he would send us some antivenene for the snakes in our area.

This antivenene finally reached the station — after a detour to snakeless New Zealand — and the Boss had to make a difficult decision.

Leo's condition was deteriorating fast but the label specified "Doctor's Use Only". If wrongly injected the result could be fatal.

The antivenene was for brown snake bite and Leo was certain it was a brown snake that had bitten her so they took a chance and administered the antivenene before bundling Leo in her blankets into the truck and heading for Cooktown hospital.

When contacted by 'phone the Cairns doctor severely reprimanded the Boss for giving the antivenene but Matron, well used to the bush, said she doubted Leo would have survived the trip to town without it.

Within a few days she was out of hospital and returned back with Norman and the mail. She had a limp for a while but her only complaint was that "Boss cut 'im too deep".

Leo was childless. Her one ambition was to get a baby — any baby — and no holds barred. Twice she had her eye on prospects from the camp in town. One was an unmarried girl and the other a mother with too many children already. Leo was sure that for "two poun' " ($4) she could realise her ambition of motherhood the easy way.

One day she nearly got her wish. A young Aboriginal girl

from a neighbouring property was left "sick" as the two station plants mustered common territory together. Despite vague mumbles from the old bachelor for whom the girl's young coloured husband worked, the cause of her "illness" wasn't hard to see.

It was evident her condition was "interesting". Leo helped explanations more by telling us with a very disgusted look that the girl had been "eating roots".

Aborigines are their own apothecaries. They know which bushes and barks yield boil-proof dyes for ultra-bright shirts; that the root of the freshwater mangrove powdered and sprinkled on the surface of the water will stupefy fish so that they can be caught in the hand and safely eaten. They boil sandalwood bark for muscular ills and pound the berries of the native quinine tree for fever. Green ants are squashed in their woven-leaf nests and sipped in water for just about every complaint and roots are used to make interesting conditions less interesting.

Leo gave the girl little sympathy. When we went down to check we'd find Leo scolding the very frightened patient unmercifully. She was only about sixteen and quite attractive. Refusing to answer questions from Ruth or me she lay rolling her eyes and moaning in a distressing way. Nor would she speak to Leo while we were there. There was nothing we could do.

It was impossible to get a truck to take her to town until the morning so we left her with instructions to Leo to stay with her and to call us if she lost the baby. We also tried to impress upon Leo to keep the baby and all its trimmings intact to take in to Matron with the girl so she could judge if the miscarriage had been complete.

As Paddy's brother Peter had died in the room adjacent to where the girl was it took considerable courage for Leo to stay with her in such close proximity to the Quinken. After Peter's death they had moved to new quarters.

As we were putting the lights out, Leo came up to make a last report. She looked a lot happier.

"I tell 'im, 'Don't you eat no more roots' and 'e say 'Alri',

Leo. You can 'ave 'im if you want 'im." Leo's face fell a bit, "But Paddy say 'No. 'e might be 'alf caste baby and make trouble all about'."

Next morning, before first light, Leo's bare feet padded up the verandah to our beds and she called softly to us.

We hurried down. The roots had worked but it would have been the answer to Leo's dream — a boy baby. She handed it to us in a shoe box, scrupulously clean and arranged with her loving care. As a guide to Matron it was hopeless so Paddy buried the tiny soul under the mango tree.

Leo came back to the house after I had gone to town in the truck with the sick girl, trying to hide her disappointment.

"Any 'ow, Ruthie, 'e 'alf caste one. 'proper pink. All a time I bin lose 'em, 'e proper grey one."

Later when the news of Leo's death filtered back from the Cairns Hospital we were both shocked and saddened. We hadn't realised her condition had been so grave. Matron, who had grown up in Leo's tribal area, told us that with Leo's death only one of her tribe survived. Measles and syphilis had taken its toll. She thought Leo's enlarged heart and early miscarriages could have been due to the latter disease.

Many times over we wished we could have kept Leo at home even if she would have ended up beside Peter on the hill. At least she wouldn't have been just another station "gin" from Up North to be buried in an over-crammed corner of an alien city cemetery.

# 5.

# OUR MELBOURNE CUP

Ruth tried hard to persuade us to be married at Laura during race week. By some logic only understood by her we'd be the first couple married there (presumably since the days of the Palmer Goldfield) "if only Jack Withers hadn't got married there first."

"If you do, all the Peninsula will be there." After some thought Ruth continued, "Everyone comes to the races!"

The postscript made the compliment a little doubtful.

Ruth spent hours planning the wedding to the most minor detail and it sounded enticing but . . . there was still the small matter of the letter Bill had yet to write to my mother so we went to Laura with nothing more than races on our minds.

In 1951 the Laura road hadn't gone more than a hundred yards or so past its turn-off from the Mareeba road so any intending race-goers from our part of the world had to go by horse.

At that time it wasn't necessary to paddock horses although it was a grassfed meet so we travelled down with the racehorses.

In addition to these Ruth and I each took one of our saddlehorses for the sports held after the meeting. We rode our selections, the part-Arabs Flash and Secret, to the races.

The Boss decided to come down with us, or rather he rode in the lead with George Watkin while we swallowed dust and dirt with our pride from our inferior position at the tail.

We had a sizeable string of horses to be raced, one of Bill's and ten from the station including one for Paddy for the Blackboys' Race at the end of each day's program. The Boss usually used this as an opportunity to try out some likely young thing for the next year's meet but usually the "boys" rode their best riding horses.

As well as Secret and Flash there were the packs to carry our clothes, swags, camp- and race-gear plus enough tucker for the road. Moses, Maureen and two others were sufficient and didn't carry big loads.

It was the best part of fifty miles to Laura so we did it in two stages. The first night out we camped on the banks of the Laura River at the Boundary Dip yards. The next day we rode into Laura and made camp.

That simply meant a tent for the ladies and a fly (a tarpaulin "roof" with no side walls) for the men and another for the tucker tent.

Paddy and Leo joined their friends at their camp.

Generously, The Pub made their showers and toilet facilities available to the campers and a vast herd of magnetic antbeds were on hand for any really urgent needs.

Water was carried by an endless chain of billycans from a small spring near which the combined native population from all stations had set up their house-keeping.

Forked sticks and a rail were cut for the assembly of billycans. Firewood was gathered by black boy and white girl while the men erected rails for saddle racks between handily spaced trees.

A yard made by wiring tea-tree rails to trees to form a rough circle with a slip-rail gate was to hold horses to be plated, brushed, beautified or merely "held". With that last refinement and a ricketty table Ruth contrived from forked sticks and saplings, our camp was complete.

Our trip down had been uneventful apart from a few minor upsets like Ruth's mare pulling away from her under rather embarrassing circumstances and one of the pack horses, the one with the tucker, rolling with her pack in an inviting sand patch.

Secret and I also had trouble with a Main Roads command car that met us in an inescapable position at the crest of the Crocodile Gap. The Main Roads chaps stopped to talk with the Boss and George in the lead and switched the motor off while they talked. They waited until the Boss had started off again before they switched on the ignition.

The horses immediately imitated mountain goats and fled to the topmost crags. I made the mistake of trying to hold my ground and Secret reared up and over pinning my leg under her.

We sorted that out and I remounted only to have the same thing happen as the men restarted the engine. This time Secret bruised the other leg. By this time Secret was in no mood to stand to be mounted and I had to call to Bill for assistance. He was used to a male society where people got busters, broke legs and/or necks, caught their own horses again, vaulted into the saddle and galloped away and seemed rather puzzled at my request to hold her head for me.

Third time lucky. I crawled into the saddle; Bill gave Secret her head and she flew up the rocks to stand with heaving sides beside Flash.

Next day the bruising came out in both legs and I looked so forlorn and stiff that the Boss gave us the day off. We spent it pottering around the camp and talking to the race-time floating population and the permanent residents at the Pub and the Police.

My quartpot which had been secured in its case on my saddle was squashed flat so I decided to 'fix' it. I fixed it permanently by forcing the soldered seam open when I tried to hammer a shoeing rasp inside the quart to open it out.

Having had one day "off" we were to report for duty and take two horses out to Olivevale, firstly to give the horses steady roadwork and secondly to borrow the tiny tent which was traditionally the jockeys' changing room at the racetrack.

Ruth had a Brave Boy mare to ride and I could scarcely believe my luck. The Boss had given me old Small Cash, a horse of equal ability whether chasing wild cattle or running in a race acquitting himself extremely well at either pursuit. For years I had admired him from a very respectful distance.

There was a drawback though. He was a tall horse and I had my doubts how I was going to get on him again once we were ready to leave Olivevale. I knew we would have an audience as everyone would be keen to inspect the Butcher Hill team.

I worried unnecessarily all through smoko as he stood like a lady's hack while I painfully dragged my bruised body into the saddle. If possible, he went up even more in my regard.

Going home we were in high spirits. We were also later than we had expected to be and decided we'd better move the horses along a bit if we were going to get to camp in time to do our chores. So we disobeyed the Boss' orders not to take them out of a trot and flew off down the bushtrack.

It was great while it lasted, feeling the controlled strength and power of our horses as they stretched out in an effortless gallop but next day we were in disgrace and our permits to train were cancelled — our horses given to Bill and Edwin. Perhaps the Boss saw the tell-tale tracks on the road or maybe someone unwittingly "dobbed us in". We'll never know.

The Brave Boy filly went shin-sore after her first start and didn't start again at the meeting but Small Cash did all that was asked of him.

Once the training of horses began, we saw very little of the men especially as we seemed to be in disgrace as far as horse-training went. Our saddle-horses were even purloined and used to take the racehorses backwards and forwards to the track, to water and to grass so we were left very much on our own.

As Bill's brother Hardy had made the trip over from Mt. Garnet to ride the Boss' horses at the meeting, his wife Iris made a very welcome addition to our camp.

Hardy and Iris had driven over in a command car, bumping along the stockroute for the last fifty miles, surveying and making their own road around trees, breakaway gullies and such bumps as were too large to go over. They had also met Edwin who was riding down on his own and after frightening the daylights out of Edwin's horse they paused while Edwin pulled his saddle from the quaking Darkie, let him go and finished the trip by motor vehicle.

The camps were mushrooming quickly around the main watering places, the spring, the Police well and the Pub so the three of us had no trouble filling in our days. Sometimes we dozed off after lunch so we could stay awake longer at night and not miss out on any of the social happenings.

Every evening after we had eaten it was customary to dress in our fanciest clothes (it was the only chance we had of showing them off) and to wend our way through the antbeds and the Pub's milking cows to the hotel verandah. Once there it was a case of ladies to the Right and Gents to the Left, to which latter direction lay the bar.

Gradually the women except for the older matrons would filter through the outskirts on the verandah and arrive at the bar too. Here the conversation was all horses. Mostly about racehorses, their weights, chances, past and future performances it was infinitely more interesting than the talk in the ladies lounge.

As is usual when ringers meet, cattle were re-mustered, bulls re-thrown and buckjumpers re-ridden. All exciting stuff and well worth the price we had to pay of drinking endless glasses of sarsaparilla offered to us as each new round of drinks was ordered.

From time to time someone would be prevailed upon to play the accordion that lived permanently on the top shelf together with the assorted bottles of spirits, a tiny wooden ladder in a narrow-necked bottle, a few mineral specimens and racing calendars and last but not least Syd Buck's finger preserved in a bottle of spirit. Syd had been parted from his finger while pulling a bore and it had become entangled in the rope.

The hum of conversation would be broken by requests to the

musicians and orders to Cecil the barman.

Bowie Gostelow could be relied on to bring his guitar with him and would play as long as there was anyone to listen to him.

If a pianist could be found or if we could inveigle the bar musicians to leave their bar stools we would dance but for the early part of the meeting all everyone wanted to do was to talk. For most, the annual race meeting was the only chance there was to talk to friends.

We had a glorious time at the races. More friends and acquaintances and the bookmakers from Cairns arrived on the old Cooktown-Laura railmotor and the Aerial Ambulance flew in to cope with accidents and injuries and to run their famous chocolate wheel to raise money to keep them flying.

The station horses won their share of the races and Bill's Blue Devil, another part-Arab and his top cleanskin-running horse, won Bill's favourite race, the Mile Off Grass.

With our hours often as late as three a.m. and as the camp was awoken without fail at five a.m., we were wrecks when the time came to ride home.

Iris rode back with us. We stayed for the sports and, with the time it takes to say 'Goodbye' to friends you couldn't expect to see for another year, it was seven p.m. when we finally left Laura.

Paddy, who had won one of the Blackboys' races, hadn't waited to watch the sports but had gone ahead with Leo to take the packs to the Boundary where we were to meet them.

The camp was the best part of thirty miles distant. Thirty miles at four miles an hour worked out at seven hours good travelling. Ruth, Iris and I didn't think we'd make it but Bill kept us going and it was two a.m. to the tick when we collapsed into our swags at the Boundary.

We were a happy party riding along the first few miles, joking and exchanging brightly coloured toffees the lucky ones had won on the chocolate wheel. Along the faintly worn pads of the drovers' road we could ride comfortably in double file.

With alarming suddenness, the rose pink sky turned to ebony and we became irresistibly sleepy as we plodded along in the darkness. Time after time, I was awoken when I rode into a low branch that scratched my face. It isn't a pleasant feeling to wake up on a horse in the middle of nowhere and not be able to either see or hear your mates. Conversation flagged as we all became sleepier.

Luckily both Bill and Ruth were riding greys and on waking I would peer hopefully into the darkness, find a moving grey shape and jog along towards it. It usually turned out to be a horse.

Ruth and Flash, both drugged with sleep, very, very nearly fell into a steep breakaway gully. Flash's sixth sense must have dulled as she had one front hoof already going down into the empty space before she plunged and struggled up again.

It was bitterly cold and we had forgotten our coats. Bill carried a square of canvas under his saddle to protect the lining from the sweat from his horse's back and although I protested feebly, I was very grateful for the protection it gave from the biting wind. Once as I dozed off, it began to fall from my clutching fingers and was sliding down Secret's shoulder when Bill checked its escape and rescued it.

We wanted to pull up and camp. Although we had no swags and tucker we argued we needed neither in our sleepy state. The stumbling blocks were our horses. We carried no hobbles and we could hardly, in fairness to them, tie them up all night. Nor could we, in fairness to ourselves, turn them loose.

In vain we waited for Bill to give the word to pull up and when we did finally reach camp, we were very pleased he had kept us going.

Towards the end of the ride the moon came up and its faint light put a faint rise in our spirits. For a short space we cantered along through the trees and half-illumined fallen logs.

The best awakening came when a tribe of wild piglets came across in front of us. For a moment neither party was aware of the other's presence. The piglets realised the danger first and began to squeal. They tangled in our horses' legs as the horses jumped this way and that trying to avoid them, grunts and squeals adding to the confusion.

Horses rudely awakened from their slumbers began to buck, scattering in all directions to get away and banging into each other — and the piglets — in their flight. We were too sleepy to realise what was happening until it was all over and the horses went along once more, warily, snorting and snuffling.

The second day's ride was a picnic. With only twenty miles to go we could afford to sleep-in past the usual five o'clock start. As we were heading for the Rodeo at Mareeba the following evening we couldn't afford to waste too much time as there were plenty of chores awaiting our arrival at the homestead.

Before we got very far along the road, Hardy caught us up in his fearful vehicle and whisked Iris, wearing the wristlet watch which was the trophy for the Ladies Bracelet, back to Mt. Garnet.

# 6.

# WEDDING BELLS

Once back from the races we spent a frenzied evening washing clothes and a more frenzied morning struggling to iron them with a temperamental petrol iron that kept bursting into flames. We needed our "town" clothes freshly laundered as we were to ride to Maitland Downs that day to join forces with Miles. He was Mareeba bound in his truck to get fencing wire and supplies and we were hitching a ride to the Mareeba Rodeo.

While Ruth cooked food to sustain the Boss in our absence Bill and I got the packbags ready. As we were travelling light we only took one packhorse loaded lightly with a suitcase of the precious "town" clothes in one bag, two swags in the other and the third swag and sundries as top load.

My swag bent in the middle willingly and was first in the packbag but Ruth's refused to bend. No matter what method we tried it resisted our attempts to get it into the bag with mine for what seemed like an hour. Then, miraculously, somehow or other, in it slipped!

We were off with waves from the others. Ralph, the packhorse, being unshod (it wasn't worth shoeing horses that normally only moved a few miles from camp to camp) wasn't terribly keen about the stony road winding up the Byerstown Range to Maitland Downs. With the three of us riding abreast behind him there was little he could do but keep plodding.

As we had finally succeeded in getting Ruth's swag into the packbag neither of us had mentioned its uncompromising nature to her but the mystery was cleared up as we followed Ralph up the range.

"Tricky fellow me," Ruth announced looking very pleased with herself and beaming at us. "I'm not going to get a sunburnt nose this Rodeo. I put my red umbrella in my swag!"

The penny dropped. But as Bill said, who, apart from Ruth, would even have thought of rolling an umbrella in a swag!

She hurriedly dug her swag out when we reached Maitland fearful that Bill and I might have damaged it with our packing methods but it came through the experience unscathed. It didn't save Ruth's nose from sunburn. She left it at a friend's house in Mareeba and there it remains.

Sitting on the hard seats in the hot sun we vowed that next year we'd do things in comfort. We'd compete and find shelter, like Bill, in the competitors' stand.

We did. The shelter was satisfactory but our performance left much to be desired. I came out the winner of the ladies Figure Eight when my fellow competitor knocked down the pegs in the finals. It was the first mistake she'd made throughout the rodeo.

It was left to Bill to uphold the honour of the Peninsula which he did by winning day money for the top score of the day plus a new saddle for the Novice Buckjump.

As he was standing selfconsciously at the edge of the arena holding the saddle to be photographed for a northern weekly a runaway buckjumper careered past. Instinctively he dropped the saddle and lunging caught the horse by its trailing halter-shank.

The reporter retrieved the saddle, dusted it down, handed it to Bill who had hoped he might have forgotten about the photograph and clicked the shutter.

After the marathon of the races, the rodeo left us feeling more dead than alive and vowing "Never. Never again." Bill, who hates travelling unless it's on horseback, complained that we should have got married while we were at the rodeo. Instead, we had to go all that way home, come back again and then still have to traverse the rough, dusty road for a third time.

To add insult to injury we all, including Miles, went home with runny noses, sore throats and splitting heads with which we promptly infected the stay-at-homes.

At least the unnecessary journeyings prompted Bill to write to my mother who, while saying I was too young — a remark which made me very indignant — gave her consent. With her blessing came a deep blue facetted Anakie sapphire of my father's. With a couple of diamond chips and a gold band it became my engagement ring.

Anything that could go wrong with wedding plans went wrong. We were still mustering and being camped-out most of the time often missed the packhorse mail that Norman brought each fortnight. It meant that it often took a month or more to answer a letter and the letters coming from both mothers, now in a firm alliance, were fast and furious.

The engagement ring on its way back from the jeweller's was sent to the Tableland farm for Bill to pick up when he had to take a trip over for medical attention. It hadn't turned up before he left to come home and after many inquiries and searches it was finally run to earth behind a wooden stay in the creamshed that doubled as roadside mailbox at the farm.

Similarly the material for Ruth's and my dresses went astray on the way to the dressmaker and barely turned up in time to have them finished for the wedding.

As we were out in the camp and thus incommunicado it didn't worry us at all but the mothers agonised over every inch of the way.

Once over in the land of the doctors Bill thought it would be a good idea if I joined him and we could be married. The idea being that it would save him a trip over That Road. Of course his letter suffered the fate of the others. He came back in the station truck with Norman before Norman had a chance to go to town to collect the mailbag containing Bill's letter and deliver it to me.

Back with them in the truck and loading came a crate with three little Tableland poddy dairy calves — the first "cattle" to be road-transported on the Mulligan Highway. Bill had bought them, two heifers and a bull for twenty-five shillings ($2.50) each to save them from the vealer man.

Ruth made them little nosebags and we reared them on pollard and buckets of watered-down molasses until they were able to fend for themselves.

Bill, vowing never again to travel the Mulligan Highway was beginning to have second thoughts about this marrying business. The Boss, aided by Norman suggested that they, both being Justices of the Peace, marry us then and there. Although it met with a fair measure of approval the legality of the arrangement was doubtful and in any event, until I aged a little, it was a case of "No mother — no wedding".

It was difficult to set a date for the wedding that would suit all concerned — especially the spayed cows for Dan Kelly, the butcher. We finally decided on December the first which seemed an easy date to remember and it would give the cows time to be mustered and droved to Mareeba without running into continuous rain to make the road impassable.

With that done the mothers were able to send out a guest list to their friends and relations who lived close handy and to arrange for a minister to marry us at the farm.

While it looked like there was only plain sailing ahead the Boss was the next problem. As my father had died the year before I was hoping the Boss would take his place and "give me away". Impossible. Field Lass was due to foal and he couldn't leave her.

She did foal while we were away and the foal was reluctant to suck. In a mistaken effort to save its life the Boss poured the best part of a bucket of water down its neck and it died. Maybe he should have come with us and left the old mare to her own devices.

We had wanted Edwin to come with us too but this was met with a plaintive "You can't ALL go!". I think he thought having a

In the droving days: Bill Wallace takes delivery of 1104 head of Merluna cattle to overland to Mareeba.

Charlie Wallace with two pretty helpers, in 1948: His daughter Ruth Shephard (left) and his daughter-in-law, Lennie Wallace (right).

The late Charlie Wallace of Butcher Hill riding Blink Bonny.

bridesmaid was a bit unnecessary too when Ruth could have been at home helping out.

However he did come up with a good suggestion. He had ordered a new tank, some gates, wire and the wet season order. Norman could take us over in the truck leaving on Thursday. That would give us Friday to get organised for the ceremony on Saturday. Sunday we could have "off" and on Monday we could pick up the tank etc. With a pre-dawn start on Tuesday we'd be back to muster the cows by the following Thursday.

This schedule also allowed for fresh horses to be shod and tucker to be cooked for the camp on the Wednesday. It sounded reasonable so the deal was clinched there and then.

Ruth and I still hadn't tried on our wedding dresses. Together with engagement ring, shoes, gloves and other paraphernalia they awaited our arrival. We were very proud that we had remembered to make an appointment at the hairdressers the day before the wedding but apart from that there didn't seem to be much else we could do.

The evening before we were due to leave the stormclouds gathered to the west. Ominously they appeared heaviest along the road we had to take and storms on that road which wasn't yet a year old meant no road at all.

Bill began his complaints again. If we had to go into Cooktown and catch a 'plane he definitely wasn't going. We would never get seats for three on the 'plane at such short notice even if Norman didn't come. We would have to go by boat. Bill refused pointblank even to consider the small coastal launch as an alternative.

He would, however, consider riding down through China Camp to Daintree, a jaunt taking several days unless the rivers came up. If that happened we could still be in the scrub somewhere until the wet ended in April or May of the next year. We turned that one down but as Bill pointed out they would have to wait for us as there was little point in having a wedding without a bride and groom!

Norman wasn't very enthusiastic about leaving. He knew the

road. He knew the truck and he knew the vagaries both of the weather and of the Boss. In the Boss's affections the Dodge was just ousted from first place by Shipmate his black thoroughbred stallion. Both had to be handled with the reverence due to the Holy Grail.

Hoping for the best the four of us set out. Norman as the only driver at the wheel with Bill beside him. We preferred the back as we both suffered from motion-sickness and hoped that the fresh air in the back would act as a preventative. Bill forcibly ejected us and made us ride in the cab through Carbine and Mount Molloy "to make it look better".

Trouble began within sight of home. The Dodge showed extreme distaste for the road normally travelled by trucks and kept slipping off into the timber. One tree in particular appeared to be strongly magnetic and it took Norman several attempts to get past it. We ran into our next problem about a mile further on at the first creek.

We went in very carefully but, despite all care, the bank crumbled under us and the truck sank, slowly and gracefully, into the bog. All that stopped Norman from reversing out and going home was that it would have been impossible. We had to go forward or not at all. It took us the best part of an hour to get out and Bill's opinion of the intelligence of people who wanted to go truck-driving in the storms wasn't very flattering.

For some time we were able to dash along at a breathtaking twelve miles an hour. Dinner was postponed until we had successfully negotiated a few treacherous little streams that had their beginnings in a line of hills just off the road. This range attracted every storm and the rivers would be bankers in next to no time. We crossed the first stream after a careful investigation on foot but as we came to the second a Main Roads command car came roaring past.

"How's the crossing?" Norm shouted over the din.

"Just sailed through," yelled the man over the gentle hum of his motor as he passed.

Two things we learnt. One, command cars are built

differently to trucks and two, you can't sail in wet sand.

We were stuck fast. Water ran through the floor of the cab and out the door Norman had left open to survey the damage. A mile or so upstream a dreadfully dark stormcloud was preparing to burst on the point of the hill. We knew for sure what would happen. The truck would be washed downstream, a total loss, and we'd be forced to flee to the Northern Territory to live out our sorry lives in exile. In a way, the latter was quite a pleasing thought for we all had a hankering to try our luck in the Territory some day.

As Norman was the only driver he took command. Ruth and I were put to work shifting huge boulders to try to alter the course of the stream. It kept us busy and out of Norman's way, which I think was the main idea. It had no visible effect on the water level.

When the men came out of conference a plan was made. Norman was to drive. Ruth and I were to push from behind and Bill was to "crank it out" by repeatedly winding the crank-handle.

We claim we did the major part of the work. Bill said his cranking was no minor component and, of course, Norman said, "Well, if it weren't for my brain, we'd still be there."

The only trouble with "cranking" as a means of locomotion is that besides being awfully hard work it is slow and uncertain. Ruth and I were giving the pushing all we had when the truck struck a submerged stone and ran along it easily for a foot or two. The shock of the sudden forward movement was so great that Ruth fell flat on her face in the water to emerge dripping and spluttering.

Directly in front of the vehicle, Bill had fortunately jumped clear so we still had a live prospective bridegroom.

A good deal more pushing and cranking and we got the truck out.

Our outsides and its insides had to be dried out before we could go on. So we trooped off, girls to one side of the river, men to the other, removed our clothes, wrung them out and put them on again. Norman dried the engine with Bill's dry shirt and we set out again, cooler at least than before our ducking.

We were now in a block of country that Bill and Miles had leased in order to muster the numerous cleanskins. They had put a couple of musters through but hadn't restocked with quiet cattle as there were still a few wild ones about. Norman had slowed the truck to a walking pace and we all had our necks craned out examining cattle tracks along the road. They were going the same way as we were and were not far ahead.

Over the next creek we caught up with them. Three young mickies, one red, one baldy and one for good measure spotted. Norman revved the engine and we chased them. They galloped along the road with us just behind them until the spotted one turned off the road and the others followed.

The truck braked to a stop. The doors flew open and the two men jumped out. Bill caught the baldy-faced mick in a gully and secured him with his belt. Meanwhile Norman was tussling with the red one. Ruth and I sat on him until the two of them downed the spotted bull. A knife was produced from one of Bill's innumerable pouches and the necessary operation to ensure the mickies' continued growth as bullocks rather than bulls, was performed.

The red fellow was last and Ruth and I started leisurely back to the truck. There was a rattle of leaves and twigs behind us but we ignored that as Norman was a great practical joker. It sounded again — closer. We walked even more slowly to show our contempt for leg-pullers.

"Look out!" called Norman and we both looked around intending to look disdainful until we saw the micky was really after us!

With his snorting breath on the tightly-stretched seats of our pants we gathered speed (that we hadn't known we possessed) rapidly, gaining the front seat of the truck together and in one bound. We sorted ourselves out later and much to the men's amusement had to get down and make our way around to our chosen seats in the back while the micky stood raking dirt over his shoulders and swearing revenge.

On we went, pulling up at the loveliest part on the road, the McLeod River, for lunch. It was really and truly that romantic spot, the oasis in the desert. Imagine travelling for hours over glaring burnt-up plains and hot, dry, little ridges where even the light timber grows knotted, gnarled and stunted for lack of anything other than stones and heat in its diet.

Then, after pushing through this and dust a foot or more deep on the road, imagine coming to a river running crystal-clear over a pebbly bar murmuring quietly to the accompaniment of birdsong from the deep green trees lining its banks. This was the McLeod, our dinner camp. It was almost worth coming all the way we had come just to sit there.

It was a lovely place and when Ruth was engaged to be married she suggested to her intended that they spend their honeymoon there. His reply was to the point. After spending most of his life in a swag he was darned (my substitution) if he was going to spend his honeymoon camped out as well.

The crossing has now been shifted further upstream and there is a bridge. It isn't nearly as tempting as the old crossing but just as well for the river-bar was showing too many touches of the human hand — empty bottles and discarded tins.

As if to welcome us to its loving bosom, the Tableland turned on a bit of its renowned weather. Hardly had we left Mareeba but the mist, drizzle and cold were upon us. Bad enough to frizzle by day without freezing by night.

Ruth and I sat and shivered in our swag-blankets in the back despite the men's invitation to share the comparative warmth of the cab.

"No thank you. We don't want to be sick," we told them. Obviously we couldn't have been suffering enough.

To make matters worse we took the wrong turn-off. Or rather we didn't take the right turn-off and kept along the main road that took us to Herberton and the blizzards. By the time this navigational error was rectified Ruth and I had jammed our persons into the front of the truck.

Our welcome at the farm wasn't at all what we had planned

even if we were a few hours overdue. As we staggered out, dusty, dirty and still wrapped in blankets from the cab of the truck, the mothers and Ruth's sister Joy, all Tableland peaches and cream, peered into the darkness trying to count the shadowy forms.

"Goodness. How many are there?"

We assured them there were no more bodies in the back and were invited in.

Once we were revealed in all our glory by the electric lights we came in for more harsh words.

"Look at their skins! They look like sand goannas!"

"And so thin and haggard!"

Considering they were all nice and freshly plump from living ladies' lives we felt it rather unjust and Bill diplomatically suggested we might like to have hot showers. We gratefully accepted and then went to bed.

Contrary to the usual Tableland weather pattern the sun shone for our wedding day and the only ripple in the calm waters was when the groom was found to be missing at daybreak. No cause for alarm — he had merely decided to give Jack a hand with the milking.

We were married in the sunny sitting room at the farmhouse. I wore a short pink frock; Ruth looked charming in blue. Bill looked uncomfortable in a dark blue suit and Jack looked unperturbed by it all. He'd been best man many times before and beat the bridegroom to kissing the bride. Mainly because three comfortable, middle-aged ladies advanced on Bill in a solid cohort, backed him against the wall to bar his retreat and became the first, collectively speaking, to kiss the 'groom.

The minister only recently arrived from England was rather in a daze. He wasn't at all happy about conducting the ceremony in a house although I told him I wouldn't have had a hope of getting the 'groom to a church.

"Why didn't you get the Bush Brothers to marry you at the homestead?" he asked.

"There aren't any."

"No Bush Brothers?" Mentally he was classing the Peninsula

with the pagan wastes of the Congo. "No men of religion at all?"

"No."

(The A.I.M., now the Uniting Church, came some two years later.)

"Who takes care of the weddings, christenings and funerals?" The poor man was quite perturbed.

I was tempted to say no one worried about the first two but thought better of it, I did tell him that the charming mother-of-the-groom did the burying at Butcher Hill.

Paddy's brother Peter had died suddenly while all the men were camped-out mustering during the Second World War. There was no one home with Peter but Mrs Wallace and old Black Charlie (also a Wallace). It was impossible for them to summon the men or the Cooktown police so they wrapped the boy in his swag cover, gathered his stockwhip and spurs and buried him on the hill with the service from the Prayer Book to guide him on his way.

They figure as undertaker and witness in the Death Register at the Cooktown Court House. Necessity is often a hard master.

• • •

A clock somewhere in the hotel chimed a quarter to four a.m. on the Tuesday morning as we left Mareeba on the way to Biboohra and home. Besides the four who had come over, there were two others going back. One was Blue, a girlfriend of Ruth's and the other my mother who would, so Ruth and I fervently hoped, eventually take over the cooking.

Added to the human cargo there were a couple of tons of loading and a bulky eight hundred gallon (4000 litres) tank. Safely deposited inside the tank was a kerosene tin packed with choice peaches from the farm, intended by the mothers to provide a change in menu at the station. Getting through the manhole of a tank while a truck is bumping along a bush road is no trouble at all if there are peaches to be gained by it. The tin was empty long before we reached home!

# 7.

# SHADES OF THE PAST

Wednesday was a rushed affair. I spent it unwrapping wedding presents and writing thank you notes and, with the help of Blue, sending off little packages of wedding cake.

Ruth spent Wednesday in a cloud of flour-dust for the plant was due to leave at daylight and we had clean forgotten to buy bread in Mareeba! The yeast bottle, sulking after being left uncared-for for a week had gone temperamental and uncooperative.

To save baking a cake we took one tier of the wedding cake with us. Bill, Edwin and Paddy put their day in shoeing fresh horses for the plant.

The spayed cows called. At daylight next morning Paddy and Leo, Bill, Edwin and I answered the call and left for the "Bottom End". Ruth and Blue went off in a Main Roads command car to some special dance in town and caught up with us later.

I loved mustering the Kennedy. It was by no means good country but it was good country to muster and, as the Boss didn't bother much about that end of the Block Fence, the odd times we did muster there made it a treat.

The Block Fence was in reality a three mile stretch of three strand barbed-wire fence strung from mountain range to mountain range across the Laura River valley. The fence, with the steep hills, effectively "blocked" homesick cattle from end of the run from returning when shifted to the other end. "Down Below the Block Fence" was a magical phrase. It meant peace and quiet forty miles from authority. We were more than forty miles from the homestead — we were in another world.

We were in a world of cliff-faced ranges, of queer convoluted conglomerate caves, of places with romantic historical associations with gold and cannibals, fearless prospectors and the earliest explorers, hordes of Chinese miners, giant pythons and lost treasure caves.

It was a world of straggling brumby bands, of the long criss-crossed trails made by the hoofs of thousands of road-cattle droved annually to Mareeba, of eroded rock-and-antbed fireplaces, of piles of horseshoes discarded by Native Police log barracks, burnt-out yards and Aboriginal art galleries as old as the moon.

It was a place where the cattle, though quiet, were few and the finding of a mob was an excitement in itself. There was also the added thrill of a chase after a marauding cleanskin bull wandered in from over the ranges. A land of enchantment.

We mustered the cows without anything unduly eventful occurring. The storms had fallen and left tiny creeks running crystal clear. There had been no floods. The grass was beginning to cover the once-brown earth with an emerald carpet and the cattle, scattered out in the hills following the storm rain, were happy and content. So were we.

Ruth and Blue loved the horses and the riding. I loved putting the cattle together in one sleek red and white mob. Bill found pleasure in both these and in burning grass.

He burnt miles of it. Each day he'd send columns of smoke spiralling up into the sky. Back at the homestead they could trace our progress by them. It is the practice in the Peninsula to burn the old dry grass to make room for the new growth. Cattle are loath to eat the old dry tussocks unless there is nothing else and then they have no feed value. It is difficult to balance a safe stocking rate with the growth of grass so fire helps out. It also destroys any seed ticks.

In the days when Australian horse breeders sold Walers to the Indian horse market, Butcher Hill, then owned by J.S. Love, was right in the thick of it. As well as running three thousand head of cattle they also grassed a thousand head of horses.

From remarks the Boss has passed I gather the breeding management was rather haphazard. Over a thousand brumbies were shot the first few years after he bought Butcher Hill and among them were some beautiful horses.

J.S. Love had a number of stallions at Butcher Hill, most of them imported horses and one of which could trace his pedigree back to a legendary "Flying Childers Mare". They were remarkably well-bred. No money was spared to buy and import them and their bloodlines are shared with the grandparents of today's turf champions. They should have produced ideal horses for the Indian market.

The mares were brought in to the stallions and when it was assured they were in foal many of them were turned out below the block fence to rear their foals. When it was necessary to muster the mares, the men rode up the Kennedy as far as they could and rode down sending anything in the gullies and smaller creeks galloping down the main water-course to the yards.

This worked well while they were dealing with the old brood mares but before long a colt foal missed in the muster grew into a stallion. Other foals missed the weaning muster and a brumby mob — with racing blood — was begun.

Legend has it that Love was not satisfied with the horses being sent down to his shipping paddocks at Egira near Charters Towers so he went to Butcher Hill to see what had gone wrong.

What he saw couldn't have been to his liking. He had all the horses mustered and run through a crush in the drafting yards. Every third horse was systematically "jugulared" (its bulging jugular vein punctured with a knife) and allowed to "bush" to bleed to death.

As one horse came in for his turn, one man called out, "That's such and such (I've forgotten his name) I'll give you twenty pounds for him."

"If he's worth twenty pounds to you, he's worth it to me," said Love and took the horse back to Townsville with him where he won several big races.

When the last horse was despatched, J.S. Love was said to have regretted that the manager was absent. He should have shared the horses' fate. Most of the horses died but one or two that were punctured carelessly survived. Bill and Paddy disinterred an unusually high number of horse bones while erecting a fence radiating from the yards. It gave credence to the story.

Before Love bought Butcher Hill it was owned by the Earl family. James Earl took it up in a series of small runs at the time of the Palmer Goldrush. With two of his brothers he had made his way from England to Victoria and through Ballarat and Bendigo to Port Denison, now Bowen.

They took up land around the Bowen hinterland and set themselves up as carriers with horse teams taking goods to the west and bringing wool back. They had a "half-way house" at Mt. Douglas on the Clermont road and in the early 1860's two of the brothers followed the race to the Plains of Promise and took up Iffley.

By this James had married a young Irish girl Marion Campbell and they set out for Iffley in the lower Gulf. Marion had a baby girl at Iffley and when the baby was only six weeks old cyclonic rain completely flooded the area. They lost all they owned, stock, improvements and personal belongings but felt, after three days in the water, that they were lucky to have escaped with their lives.

Both James and his brother were strong swimmers and one helped Marion while the other pushed the baby in a cradle made waterproof by covering it with berkmyre. Somehow they got back to the property they still owned west of Bowen, Yackamunda.

Before they had time to get really depressed about their loss gold was discovered at Ravenswood and the brothers were back in business carting for the goldfields and supplying Yackamunda bullocks to the hungry miners.

Charters Towers followed Ravenswood, then the Palmer and James took a load of provisions and a small herd of cattle to the Palmer. He was still looking for a home of his own and climbing the ridges that led from the Palmer to the top of the Byerstown Range he saw the Laura Valley below. He decided to take it up and he called the aggregation of small blocks he selected "Butcher Hill" after their English home in the Fens.

The Boss's mother Isobel Earl, came to Butcher Hill as a small child taking turns in riding the pony with her sister who was born at Iffley and alternatively riding in the dray with her mother and baby sister and brother.

She married Charlie Wallace a great horseman and a packer to the Normanby field and spent most of her life around or in Cooktown. When the Earl family bought Butcher Hill back from J.S. Love they offered it for sale again and Isobel's two sons Arthur and Charlie bought it. Later Charlie (the Boss) held it in his own right. He had been there over twenty years when we were married and had rebuilt it into one of the top properties in the area.

During the days of the Palmer a road — or a pack-track — used to come from Cooktown on the coast to Butcher Hill. There one track branched off and crossed the range to what used to be Byerstown and Uhrstown. Another track led up the Normanby to the workings and batteries there and a third led down the Laura River to below where the block fence now stands. There it turned up a creek into the hills and dropped over into the Maytown fall.

This road was in one way better travelling than the first one but the gap in the hills was the notorious Hell's Gates and few people would like to travel knowingly the road that led through the Gates of Hell. It derived its name from the natives' unpleasant habit of ambushing lonely travellers at this pass. It was an easily discernible gash on the hill-face making any traveller on it visible to the watching natives.

It was a natural trap. With a road block at either end, a cliff face going up on one side and down on the other very few lone wayfarers got through if the natives were hungry.

The natives were not interested in gold or the possessions the men, white and Chinese, had with them. The old miners theorised that the bodies were taken to a cave, of which there are many in the area, and prepared there using the man's swag and other belongings as fuel for the cooking fires. They gave the name of Devil's Kitchen to this cave and though many looked for it and the gold it must reveal no one has found it.

The Kennedy caves are more benign. They are conglomerate with blowholes and pillars, doorways, arches and vaulted ceilings of waterworn pebbles cemented together with a pastel-toned mortar. They are untenanted except by rock wallabies, dingoes and an occasional wild pig and are well worth the climb up the hill to see them.

Higher up the Kennedy the country flattens out and there are springs.

Here the Chinese made their gardens. On some of the other creeks which join the Laura below the Kennedy junction, scattered mango and citrus trees with a few old posts bear witness to the existence of the men who gardened for the miners.

In the hills on the Maytown side, the old mine-shafts are still open to sun and sky. The poltergeist that once panicked the horses and chased the Chinese miners from Cannibal Creek has ceased his practical jokes.

What was once the Wild Irish Girl, the England Forever, the Last Chance or the Lone Star are now just a scattering of charred posts, some rusty tins and a lot of holes in the ground. But the shades of the old miners are still there and so, say the old-timers, is the gold.

# 8.

# IN THE TRACKS OF THE MINERS

The Normanby, another part of the old Palmer goldfield, was also on our mustering list. Quiet cattle drifted up the river in search of green picking and water in the dry months. When rain fell they had to be mustered and brought back home again. Any wild bulls found with the branded cattle were usually shot on sight and the cattle taken back to the station yards.

The American hamburger market for Australian bull beef had yet to open and bulls were unsaleable. They were "bad" bulls, quick to charge, very big and not really worth the risks involved to turn them off as stags in two or three years time.

Calves were branded, saleable stock held for sale and the rest turned bush again. While the grass was good down the river they would hang around close to the homestead but when the green feed was in short supply they'd head off back up the river once again. Each year meant a repeat performance.

Mustering upriver was difficult. Besides the chance that cleanskins would send the quiet cattle — and themselves — galloping out of the river and into the hills at our approach, the country was extremely rough. There, miles were measured standing on end.

Added to this were the hazards of the gold days. The country was riddled with gaping holes and some almost bottomless shafts.

The first time I went up there, the warning "Watch out for mines" didn't sink in until my pony propped dead on top of what I thought was a weather-beaten antbed. When I saw the depth of the hole on the other side of the heap of dirt I decided to keep my eyes open a bit wider.

One creek was an old Chinese diggings. The Chinamen were allowed to work only alluvial gold. Reefs were not for them. However, they found enough of the alluvial. No one knows the amount of gold that was smuggled out to China but smuggling was so rife that the bones of dead Chinese miners were hollowed-out, filled with gold dust, placed in the traditional burial urns and shipped home to China. Here both the bones and their contents were well received.

Though much has been said about Chinese miners no aspersions can be cast on their working ability. I have been told how they emptied a small lake by the monotonous method of bailing the water out by the bucketful and tipping it elsewhere. Prospect Creek is a fitting tribute to their industry. The complete length of the creek has been worked back some fifty yards or more from its banks. The creekbed received the fine-tooth treatment.

During the dry season every stone was removed from the bottom of the creek and pitched neatly to make a stone wall against the banks. When the water came down in the Wet a fresh layer of alluvium was left in the cleaned creek bed. This was washed for gold.

Like the Kennedy the Normanby was rough and rugged, even more so, and held a strong attraction for me. No one had to twist my arm to get me up there. Perhaps the best trip I had was when we went up with Miles to erect a series of yards.

Miles' property Maitland Downs bordered on the Normanby and a considerable number of his cattle were suspected of straying that way. We hoped to use the yards to muster the cattle for Miles to take back.

It was storm-time before we were free to go up there and no matter how early we climbed from our swags the rain seemed to beat us to the next camp. We kept going upstream past the country we usually mustered and into the unknown territory where the river headed. It was to be a clean-up muster to end all musters.

Travelling single-file up the riverbed or cutting corners by going over the hills was rather eerie. We hadn't been that way before and several times we had to turn back to try another route when access was blocked. There were no real tracks just a few faint cattle-pads leading to the main water-holes.

These pads were very narrow and often the branches were too low to permit the horses to pass, let alone the riders. They had to be cut from time to time with the hornsaws the men kept on their saddles so that we could continue.

Often when scaling hillsides it would be too steep to ride and we would dismount and lead our horses, skidding down the other side dodging horses and the stones they, in turn, dislodged.

Once when Bill and I were riding in the lead of the Indian file, he carrying a rifle in case of wild bulls, we successfully negotiated a narrow pad where a washout had all but eroded the narrow pad. At the outside edge there was a drop of a hundred feet or more to a rocky creek-bed. We had gone some distance past this place when there was a shout and the rattle of falling stones. Robert the packhorse had gone over.

I didn't like to look and went on until the rest of the horses were on more or less level ground and held them there. Bill had gone back with the rifle and I was expecting to hear at any moment the shot that meant poor old Robert was delivered from his sufferings.

It never came. Robert's life was saved by a horse-collar and two trees. Although he wasn't one of the horses used to snig posts and rails for the yards he, as the quietest horse, carried the horse-collar.

When he fell down the bank rolling several times he became caught between the two trees. These stopped his long descent and the big padded collar saved his neck.

It took some time to extricate him and get him safely back to the pad. He was unpacked and the various pieces had to be carried

Station mothers dress in their best for the Coen races of 1958: The late Ruth Shephard, Iris Wallace, and Lennie Wallace, with young Billy.

Putting the billycans on Maureen the 'tucker' horse. A pack cover covers the bags because of a likely storm.

Drovers Lennie and her friend "Blue" have a rest at the McLeod River.

The mob "on-the-road", viewed from "the tail", with 400 miles to go.

piece by piece up the steep bank. Then Robert himself was led up.

He was not seriously hurt but was badly shaken and probably had a few strains and sprains. He was too wobbly on his feet to be packed for a few days so another horse carried his load. He stuck to his collar though and we were all more wary of bad washouts after that.

The hills were quiet. The few cattle we sighted we left undisturbed. Occasionally we saw an old bull forced from the mob and feeding alone on a high hill-top. As our beef supply couldn't keep up to the appetites of Bill, Miles, me and three blackboys our diet was often supplemented with bull-beef. Although it isn't a recommended diet, especially if you have to run your dinner for a couple of miles before you can shoot it, bull-beef is certainly better than no beef.

When you become used to it you don't notice the stronger flavour as much. We usually took tail and kidneys for stew, fried the fillet in the camp-oven and roasted or boiled the rumps. This way it wasn't too tough or too highly spiced with masculinity.

The cuts usually roasted were salted down and the dogs had next call on the carcass. When they had finished it was the wild pigs' party.

By the time the last yard was built I had gained a range of camp-cookery experience. I couldn't turn out featherlight sponges from the cast-iron camp-oven but I did make recognisable scones and apple tart made with the dried apple we carried. A great improvement was using compressed yeast that Miles contributed for the bread baking. As far as I was concerned the do-it-yourself yeast bottle would become a thing of the past.

I learnt the subtleties of starting a fire in pouring rain. Dead sticks still adhering to trees were very much drier than ones garnered from sodden ground. I confirmed that matchwood, if available, is the be-all and end-all of a firelighter's existence. Even if wet it seemed to burn readily with a bright flame. Some call it "Kerosene" wood.

At the expense of a scorpion-bitten finger I learnt that it is best to look carefully before picking up wood from the ground. I found that externally wet stumps when splintered with an axe yielded dry tinder and I learnt the hard way that the brim of your hat can act as guttering and downpiping and will extinguish the bravest fire if you bend too far over it in a downpour.

After trying to cook bread (unsuccessfully) in waterlogged camp-oven holes I experimented with hanging the oven over a mild fire and placing the usual coals on top of the lid. Sam the prospector had told me that if you can just stand the heat on your hand held under the suspended oven the temperature is right. It was. I also became a professional in erecting shaky galleys of saplings and sheets of bark peeled from obliging trees to house my fires.

Apart from seeing that there was enough tucker cooked for three meals a day and taking smokos to the men as they worked I had no other chores.

One camp had been an old mining camp too and fossicking about amongst the rusty debris, sheets of iron, broken cast-iron cooking vessels, cans and bottles I found a Chinese pottery jar. It was roughly spherical, extremely light and apparently flameproof as it showed signs of having survived at least one bushfire. At the top was a small opening and a smaller spout jutted from one side. I took it home safely wrapped in my swag.

While digging a drain around his tent Miles unearthed a quaint silver lid. Embossed on it was a mounted horseman with flying banners and around it was a circle of what looked like Greek lettering. Miles gave it to me for Ruth.

Wheels from ubiquitous wheelbarrows turned up frequently and we took two upon which we built our own barrows. If the miners pushed them loaded with their gear from the last goldfield they certainly needed medals for perseverance — or psychiatric treatment.

At a camp downstream one of the Butcher Hill men found a rusty revolver and hung it in the tree supporting the poles of the tucker-tent. We speculated on its history. Had it belonged to a miner who kept it to protect both himself and his gold? Or had a stockman carried it in the days when the area was part of a State-owned cattle station? It hung there for years until a "boy" employed casually took a fancy to it and it disappeared.

The yard was to be erected on the river flat opposite the one where I found the Chinese pot. While snigging rails for the yard Bill discovered a pig nest in the long grass and a newly-farrowed litter inside. The camp was divided as to whether they should be destroyed or not but their newness saved them.

They were only about a day old and as the mother kept warily away I was able to admire them. I was wary, too, and if any piglet made distress sounds I'd be up and gone in a split-second!

There were six of them, three completely black and three little fellows striped horizontally like watermelons. They were very friendly and would snuggle up to be petted and played with. The nest was made of long grass with the centre hollowed out and arranged to make grass walls and a roof high enough for the sow to lie with the piglets without destroying the camouflage.

Bill shot two bulls, one above and one below the camp so meals were assured for the piglets for days to come. We shifted before the breezes became too aromatic.

We followed the old bullock-wagon road down the river. The cuttings the old hands had made were remarkably well preserved. Stone-pitching reinforced the walls and logs placed strategically prevented the gullies from eroding too badly. Tons of machinery were brought into the Normanby diggings and each piece came by bullock- or horse-wagon or by pack-team. The Chinese community made use of their numbers and had a human carrier system at the jog. Miners' belongings were traditionally wheeled in a barrow but it most certainly wasn't suitable wheelbarrowing terrain.

Many of the climbs that had to be made by the wagons were very steep. By necessity freight charges were high but it is little short of miraculous that they were able to get the bulky stuff — the great steam boilers, pumps and stampers — in at all.

Exorbitant prices were asked for everything used by the miners. One packer is reputed to have paid their weight in gold for a horse-shoe and nails to reshoe a horse from his team. And made up the price he paid in that horse's first load.

Two gold batteries are left on the Normanby. One is just a wreck with only its steam boilers left stranded like beached whales on the river flat. The other is a going concern. Underground water troubled all the mines. It turned up sooner or later in every shaft sunk. In those days the pumps weren't as efficient as they are now and mining once the water had been reached became an arduous task.

Moreover, the men didn't like working with pumps and it was an industrial dispute and call for more pay that closed the top battery. The manager had his orders for the men to be paid off and the pumps pulled up. That done he left. A big rock python caretakes for the English shareholders.

The Boss was never idle for long by Normanby waters. He'd use his quart-pot cup as a gold dish to wash the sands for gold. At times he did find a few specks but he lost them while waiting for the next lot to turn up so it wasn't really profitable.

His father and uncle had both operated pack-teams during the golden era coming to the Palmer from the Northern Rivers district of N.S.W., a district renowned for its good horsemen. Like many others who know the field he believes there is still gold there in payable quantities.

He told Ruth and I about the miner who was supposed to have buried his pickle bottle of gold-dust in an antbed for safe-keeping. And then couldn't recall which antbed it was. He knocked down thousands of them before he was taken away to an institution.

Perhaps someone else found the gold. We didn't though we found plenty of pickle bottles. Apart from the bottles that contained the variety of alcoholic drinks, pickle and sauce bottles were in the greatest supply. The Boss told us that, in those days before refrigeration, most meat usually went slightly "off" if not consumed immediately after slaughter and the condiments were to disguise the rancid taste.

The first time I ventured up the "wild" Normanby I was looking forward to the experience but I was scared stiff. Ruth had told me many vivid horror stories about wild bulls and their ways and gave me endless advice on what to do should the cleanskins appear to be getting the upper hand. It was quite incidental that she had never been to the Normanby nor, indeed to where the really ferocious cattle were.

Still she told a good tale and I was terrified when Bill left me with a charging cleanskin cow at least as big as my pony, Laura, and told me not to let her get away while he galloped off after a bull. The contempt in which Peninsula folk held cowards was in conflict with my desire not to become a dead hero.

Of course, the old cow sensed my lack of courage and decided to try me out. She may have had me summed up correctly but she made a bad mistake about Laura. When the cow advanced with her long sharp horns at the ready, Laura merely side-stepped and bumped her with all the force available to her at the point of the cow's shoulder.

Laura's confidence buoyed mine and we soon had the cow bluffed and were still in control when Bill returned. However the cow was adamant that she was not going to move even when her mates milled around her and were quite willing to be driven back to the yard.

She threw herself down and flatly refused to get up. Bill said she was an old rogue and had done this on another occasion and they had been forced to leave her behind.

This time after trying to get her back on her feet he walked around behind Laura and to the amazement of both horse and rider pulled some long hairs from her tail. To my questions he didn't reply but produced his knife, ear-marked the cow, sawed the sharp tips from her horns with his horn-saw and proceeded to spay her.

The horsehair was used as twine to suture the incision. We rode off and left her where she was lying at the edge of a small water-hole. I didn't expect to see her again — post-op shock and all that — but she turned up the next year, tractable and fat as a seal and was duly sent off with the spayed cows to Dan Kelly, the Mareeba butcher.

# 9.

# FRIDAY START

The Boss was a superstitious man. Of course, he denied it but there was no way he would commence a journey on a Friday. That was taboo. Should his business be of extreme importance he would make a start on Thursday night camping a few miles along the road. In that way he would be continuing Thursday's journey and not starting a new one on Friday!

To Bill, one day was as good as another and one muster we left for the "wild" Normanby on Friday. The Boss must have been away for it to happen and we hadn't gone far when things began to go wrong.

First of all, Robert the packhorse missed the shallow river crossing and fell into a deep hole submerging the packs. Robert of course carried the flour. Then the gear began to break and Ruth's swag almost got a ducking in another water-hole when a top-strap securing it broke.

Bill was riding in the lead dropping matches into the old grass. Ruth and I were behind with Stan, Norman's younger brother and a particular friend of Ruth's at the time. It was very hot and the heat and smoke from Bill's fires, though gratifying to him, was not appreciated by those riding behind.

The horses didn't like it either as a fire suddenly shot up in a patch of dry grass at their feet and the cane-grass cracked like a rifle shot beside them. They zig-zagged all over the countryside.

Looking at the loads I thought the strap that secured the billycans was dangling. I voiced my suspicions to Ruth buth she and Stan were talking and she said everything looked O.K. to her.

Then, in the burning grass ahead there was a strange sight that proved to be the smallest billycan complete with its sugarbag stuffing that had been jammed between the cans to stop rattles. The bag was blazing merrily.

"Look! Billycan!" I called, pointing to it.

"You can save it," Ruth agreed without looking away from Stan. We were collecting gear. Ruth was saving for her own droving plant and I was scavenging for Bill and myself.

"But it's OUR billycan," I expostulated trying to make her see sense.

"Righto," Ruth replied in the tone that adults use towards stupid children. "It's yours and Bill's."

By this Stan had come into our conversation.

"It's our billycan", he announced in measured tones.

"For heavens sake! Let them have it. . .". Daylight dawned. "It's our CAMP billycan! Quick someone! Do something before the solder melts."

Stan and I were off our horses and trying to retrieve it from its funeral pyre with my whip. In the meantime Ruth had caught the billycan horse and found to her horror that only the biggest, the beef billy, was left. We got Bill to stop the horses and spent a half-hour tracking down the rest of the set in the grass. We found them in the long grass for the horses avoided the fire where possible.

Edwin and Paddy rejoined us. The billycans were secured and we followed up the main river. Around the first bend was a lovely big river flat covered with Townsville lucerne and sweet summer grasses. It was a favourite spot for cattle and often a cleanskin bull grazed there with the branded stock.

Today was no exception but as soon as he sighted us he left the mob at the gallop. He was absolutely enormous and almost dwarfed the others. Bill swung around trying to head him with the other men attempting to push the other cattle up to him in a compact mob. Ruth and I were left with the horses.

We decided to move them along slowly the way we were already heading towards camp. In the distance we could hear a melee of galloping hoofs, whip cracks and an occasional yap from a dog. Being curious, we pushed the horses on a little faster.

As we went off to follow a creek up, our peace and our horses were scattered by two galloping horsemen, two dogs and the bull. They bailed him up in a position that made our situation very awkward to say the least. Strung out in a long line our horses presented an ideal target to an enraged bull and we could recall too many stories of bulls disembowelling plant horses to make us feel really confident. It was a case of "This could happen to you", and we weren't happy with the thought.

For minutes that seemed hours the men played tag up and down the creek with the bull while Ruth and I surreptitiously gathered the horses in to us with what we hoped was an escape route up the creek. Then with a roar and a bellow the bull broke out and raced back down the creek, dogs hanging to him and men galloping alongside to keep him going in the right direction.

Edwin and Paddy had the coachers in exactly the right position and by the time we had caught up with the horses both the coachers and the bull were safely yarded at the camp.

After a hurried cup of tea they decided they'd rope the bull and remove the sharp tips of his horns both to make him more managable and to stop him injuring the other cattle in the yard.

The plaited greenhide ropes were big cumbersome things of varying sizes. The headrope, the strongest, was of four strands of thick greenhide, a sturdy rope almost an inch thick. On the end of it was a heavy iron ring through which the rope was passed to make a loop. The leg ropes were a fraction lighter and little shorter but very strong.

Ruth and I stopped on our horses in the wing of the yard and on a small rise. We were supposed to be keeping an eye on the cows with baby calves that had been left outside the small railed yard. In the minutes that followed we wouldn't have noticed if they had all vanished.

The four men were on foot. They hung around the outside of the rails while the bull came snorting to them, coming so close with only the rails between them that he blew saliva and froth over them. We didn't know why Bill didn't shoot the bull when we first saw him but both he and Stan were keen to "bring him back alive" as he really was mammoth.

At last, working over the rails, Bill looped the rope over the bull's head. Eager hands helped him wrap it swiftly about a strong growing tree and the four of them pulled and heaved trying to pull the bull up short against the tree. The bull didn't like the idea and resisted whole-heartedly. At one escape attempt he wrenched the rope through their burning hands and charged off through the cattle trailing the thirty feet of rope after him.

Bill and Stan jumped in to re-secure him and while one deliberately provoked the bull to charge him over towards the snubbing tree the other nimbly seized the trailing end of the rope, jumped through the rails and had the slack twisted around the tree as the bull's huge head crashed against the rails.

The men seemed to be enjoying themselves with a ton or so of bull trying to get loose to even the score. They could even laugh at the jokes they made when the bull just missed one of them in a headlong rush.

Outside, comparatively safe on our horses, we felt rather sick just watching, but we were anchored there.

As the bull lunged on the end of the rope his superior weight and strength sometimes gained him a foot or two of rope but as he threw himself around the men patiently reeled him in, inch by inch, until he was breathing spit and fire over them once more. Then, with the other three leaning back on the headrope Edwin slipped through the rails to put on the first leg-rope.

He didn't make it. Catching sight of Edwin Gostelow the bull kicked out and lunged. The iron ring snapped sending both pieces far over the yard into the bushes. The bull was free. Edwin dropped his rope and streaked for the rails. Just as he was about to vault the rails he paused a fraction of a second to see where the bull was.

The bull was right on him and Ruth and I shut our eyes to avoid seeing a mate trampled to death but when we opened our eyes, by some miracle Edwin had gained the top rail as the bull crashed into the post under him, grazing Edwin's leg as he charged.

Stan and Bill jumped simultaneously into the yard and in the split second the bull took to notice his new targets, Edwin slipped over the rails to safety.

Ruth and I had seen enough. We were at the rails to meet Stan and Bill when they ducked out again. Couldn't they just shoot the bull?

They laughed. But Bill confessed later that while the bull was almost upon Edwin he was trying to think how on earth we'd manage to get Edwin (or his body) out. Already there was one grave up there near the camp. We didn't want to add to it.

Finally Bill remounted Pidgeon and rode into the yard. Slowly he took his revolver from the holster and checked the cartridges. The first shot he fired hit the bull direct on his broad forehead. The bull shook his head and retreated. After that he took good care not to present his head full-on to the man on the horse. He didn't charge as much but tried to dodge in amongst the others. If Bill edged up to him he'd snake away, a very elusive target.

After a couple of near-misses from the bull's horns Pidgeon wasn't too keen on getting really close, either. Finally Bill decided he'd let the bull outside and gallop alongside for a heart shot.

They manouvered the bull out of the dropped rails and, once in the open he didn't go far, much to our relief. He got no further than the wing when he dropped dead with a shot behind the shoulder.

Ruth and I had often talked of buying ourselves a revolver each to carry on our saddles. That way, we figured, we'd be safe from anything that crossed our paths in anger.

When the bull's bones had been picked clean and bleached

we retrieved his skull to hang on a sapling in the wing as was customary with memorable "wild" ones. We gave up all thoughts of buying revolvers when we saw the four evenly spaced bullet holes in the wide forehead!

# 10.

# 'POSSUMS UP A GUM TREE

After such a good beginning to our "Friday start" muster we set out next day with coachers to muster up-river. We had just left our camp in time, too. Bill shot another bull, downstream this time, after it had first raced through the tucker tent and emerged with a pack-bag looped on one horn. Luckily it came free before it was taken too far and very little damage was done.

Except that there wasn't enough flat country for cowboys to gallop over endlessly, as is their habit, the Normanby would make ideal technicolour western country. There was scenery and beautiful cliffs over which the "baddie" could fall to his death and rocky, swirling river currents from which a heroine in distress could be rescued.

In one place we had to ride along the river itself for quite some distance as the stream ran through solid rock walls which rose up straight from the water's edge on either side. Rock wallabies, tails up, bounded from ledge to ledge and scuttled into crevices at our approach.

An eagle and his mate soared high above and we could see their nest, an untidy arrangement of sticks at the top of the highest tree on the uppermost point of the cliff. We felt as free as the eagles. The rest of the world need not have existed for all it mattered to us.

Bill left Edwin with us to ride in the lead while he and the other two men left the river to scout out around the creeks and hills. We were to wait where one creek flowed into the main stream.

As we were going along towards the end of the solid rock walls a cow and calf suddenly cut across the water and vanished. Ruth went after them floundering over the rocks but there was no sign of them. Tracks don't show up too well on rocks. Edwin came back from the lead to try his luck but it wasn't his day either.

We couldn't waste too much time as we would have to get to the rendezvous in case the musterers came in with cattle. Edwin told us the cow was a noted rogue and running in this part of the river she knew every inch of it and every escape route.

Just before we came to our appointed meeting place we heard a bull bellow from the hill above us. A young two- to three-year-old bull came down calling to the coachers. In the thick scrub behind him we saw three more cattle, a big, old bull, a young micky and a bullock.

The young bull wasn't a bad type, a white-faced Hereford. Probably his mother was a branded cow and he had been missed as a calf. He came down the slope to within yards of our cattle and stood.

The others weren't as curious as he was. After a second look they broke from the shelter of the scrub and racing down-hill in front of us disappeared into the river. Ruth and I pushed the coachers up quickly and managed to bunch them around the two younger bulls for the micky had stayed with his mate. We had two to make up for the two we had lost — if we could hold them. It made us feel a bit less guilty.

Edwin threw the bullock and tied him up on a small quinine-covered flat just around the bend from where he left us. While chasing the old bull he met Paddy coming to find us, so joining forces they threw the old bull and tied him down not far from the bullock.

He was a big fellow though not as big or as muscular as Edwin's friend of the yard. This bull, said Edwin, must have been "hopping mad" as he kept getting up and trying to chase them with his legs tied by the bull-strap.

They decided to tie his forelegs as well. An action usually frowned upon as a beast struggling to rise and tied both behind and in front can quite easily break a shoulder. In any case few animals tied down that way are fit to travel after being left for any length of time.

Paddy was going back to look for Ruth's cow and calf so they decided to leave the bull with both straps until Paddy returned. Then the front strap would be released. Edwin returned to us after they had de-horned both animals and relayed Paddy's message. We were to wait for Bill and Stan at the junction as planned but a hundred yards or so up the creek rather than in the main stream.

Off we went, and waited and waited and waited. We could hear galloping and dogs and whips and a very occasional shout. Up and down the riverbed they went apparently trying to get something out from the river and into our coachers waiting in the creek. Edwin left us. We edged the coachers closer to the junction to act as decoys but the men had gone again from earshot. Our two cleanskins were tiring of our company and were eager to be off.

Finally Stan appeared with a bleeding cut above one eye. It looked rather frightening but the amount of blood was really disproportionate to the size of the injury. They had been chasing a piker bullock when it fled down a steep, high bank. Bill went after him and Stan, reasoning that where two could go a third could follow, sent his mare after them. His mare turned a somersault on the way down cutting Stan's forehead and skinning her own. A few stones dislodged in the manoeuvre bounced from various parts of Stan's — and Margie's — anatomy but did no major damage.

Bill and the bullock were gone by the time Stan had re-mounted but, tracking them, he came upon them further downstream. The piker bailed up and refused to go. Not even the combined effort of Snowy on his nose and Growler on his heels would shift him but a bullet through the soft cartilage of his nose did and that was when we heard them galloping once again in the river-sand. We took the coachers out to them.

Stan exchanged his tired mare for Ruth's fresher mount and helped us with the coachers. Bill and the dogs were there with a long-headed, wild-eyed old piker with strings of saliva hanging from his mouth. Somewhat incongruously, he was half-sitting in a small pool of water, looking from a distance like Ferdinand under his favourite cork-tree smelling the flowers.

Bill's horse was knocked-up too and had blood on its side where the piker's horn had grazed his ribs. Naturally we swapped horses. Trying to get a walk out of Devil I wondered how on earth he had so recently been galloping and propping, climbing cliff-faces and handling heavy river sand. He was dead on his feet. Devil was the horse that had won the Grassfed Mile for us at Laura.

Even with the coachers milling around him, some actually sniffing him, the old bullock refused to get up. He was given another chance in the next muster but didn't take advantage of it and had his throat cut. No more would he lead quiet cattle out of the river and up into the hills at the sound of hoof-beats.

One glance at our mob was enough to tell Bill we had lost the cow and calf. We hung our heads in suitable shame but pointed out in our defence we had the bull and the micky to take their place. That didn't appease Bill. Cattle put into a mob were to be kept there. We were in disgrace.

We stopped on our way downstream to get the bull from the quinine patch. Paddy had forgotten to untie his forelegs! He came about a hundred yards with us and collapsed. Next day when someone went back to check, he was dead.

The other one proved little better off. He had kicked himself from the shade into the glaring sun and although he did recover we were unable to take him home that muster. That made the score two short as we didn't get the cow and calf again that muster either.

When we came to the place where the baldy fellow had come into the mob he had a change of heart and wanted to leave but we managed to keep him. As it was getting dark Ruth and Paddy went on ahead, Ruth to see to the cooking and Paddy to bring the spare horses in and hobble them close to the camp.

We struggled on in the darkness yarding up by moonlight.

Though no one heard anything during the night, the next morning the Hereford was gone. No broken or loose rails. He must have jumped. The little one was still there looking even smaller and more under-sized amongst the other cattle. The escapee was seen once more that year when we weren't mustering and hasn't been seen since. Maybe he left for quieter pastures.

So much for a Friday's start.

Ruth was cook for the Friday-Start muster and each evening as she came in she would tie her horse in a convenient place in case another bull rampaged through the tucker-tent.

The last evening at the camp Bill said I could go in early too as the cattle were then no trouble to yard. To show how fearless we were we let our horses go in hobbles and within minutes they were in the creek and out of sight.

It was a picture of domestic bliss. Ruth was putting the last touches to the rice and stew and I was sitting barefooted in the tent mending a torn shirt of Bill's. All was at peace.

Then we heard the alarm noises — galloping hoofs, dogs, whips and yelling men — all gaining in crescendo and coming our way. The hair stood up on the backs of our necks.

I scaled Bill's rolled swag and an antbed in one leap and reached the riding-saddle rack at the same time as Ruth. Without a word we looked it over and found it wanting. We veered to the pack-saddle rack but it didn't look very strong — or very high — either.

Together we ran to a small crooked tree with very rough bark and a convenient fork about four feet up from the rocky ground.

I got there first and gave Ruth a leg-up. She managed to catch her booted foot sideways in the fork and couldn't get the other foot from the ground.

The thundering hoofs had made a circle, crossed the creek

Lennie Wallace with her favourite stock horse, Ranger.

Bill Wallace enjoying a spot of steer riding at Mareeba Rodeo in the 'fifties.

Drovers build a canvas boat to cross the Laura River in flood, 1958.

and were nearly upon us. There was still plenty of yelling and occasional yapping. It would have to be that big bull they got yesterday, we decided.

Spurred on to action, Ruth pulled harder at her foot and I pushed from below. She was on the first branch! But I couldn't get up until she reached the next branch. The action was getting closer and I was making impatient moves at the foot of the tree.

"Wait till I get my boots off," pleaded Ruth tugging and trying to hold her precarious position at the same time. Much pulling and tugging but the boots remained on.

"I'll have to take my leggings off first," she apologised. There was more exertion from the bottom limb, the noises were right behind us but Ruth was still perched on that crucial lower limb.

"Blow that!" I retorted and pushed upwards just missing her boot on its downward descent.

Hardly had I curled my second leg beside me when they came past within feet of our tree — Stan, Snowy, Growler and the little blind steer from the coachers.

We tried our hardest to look like bits of tree bark. We didn't succeed. Stan was grinning from ear to ear as he passed guiding the steer back to the yard with something he could react to — noise.

That wasn't the end of it. We couldn't get down. In the finish I jumped and skinned an elbow on the rough bark. Somehow Ruth scratched her bare foot with the spur on her booted foot and ended in a tangle on the ground.

Naturally, the story lost nothing in the telling. Our reputation as cowgirls was irretrievably gone.

# 11.

# THE CURRAGHMORE MARE

Race-time had come around again once more and the Boss had to go to the Tableland farm on business. Ruth accompanied him on pleasure. On their way over they were to call at Curraghmore Station to select a mare to go back with Miles' droving plant to Butcher Hill where she was to join the string of race-horses for the Laura and Cooktown meetings.

When they arrived at Curraghmore, the men were late with the horses and it was almost dark before they got them into the yards. Nothing daunted, the Roberts with the Boss and Ruth set off to select a horse by torch-light.

The mare they picked was a classy brown mare with a narrow blaze and a luxuriant blue-black mane — Souvenir. She was kept back in the night paddock to be handed over to the drovers and the others were turned out again before the race-enthusiasts left.

Meanwhile we at Butcher Hill were entertaining — or were being entertained by — Roy, a saddler by trade, who was repairing the station saddles. Roy liked station life and Curraghmore was his adopted home. Consequently when Souvenir arrived in the company of another Curraghmore horse, Roy greeted them as long lost friends and their welfare became his foremost concern.

The hose was taken from where I had it running on the rows

of tomatoes and was next seen connected to the tap at the saddle-shed at one end and to Roy's hand at the other.

Souvenir was hosed and rubbed and hosed and rubbed again until the water ran from her coat crystal clear and she was left lustrously sleek. A broken wind-up gramophone spring became a scraper to remove excess water and a scuffle with the inner mysteries of Roy's huge box of gear produced a pair of horse brushes which Roy soon put to energetic use. The curious onlookers were shooed away but when Roy considered Souvenir was ready to do Curraghmore proud, and he also, indirectly, we were summoned to appear and inspect.

She looked beautiful. Whereas before she had been merely a good sort of a horse in top condition now she looked every bit of a thoroughbred mare bred to race. She carried herself like a queen too and moved proudly with the hint of muscle rippling under the sheen as she was paraded for us.

Roy waited for the compliments and we obliged with the ones we thought would please him the most.

Ruth being absent I led.

"You can't tell me that mare isn't corn fed."

Souvenir had been brought over for the grass fed meeting.

"You're telling me," Edwin Gostelow agreed. "You don't get that sort of shine from grass."

Bill, of course, made no comment.

Roy took the bait and hotly denied the mare had been fed.

"She always looks like that. She's a good doer that one." He told us two or three times for emphasis. All the same, his chest was swelling with pride over our accusations. He knew they were made in fun and he took them and rightly so as compliments to his well-loved Curraghmore and its horses.

Roy had been with us about a week when Edwin broke his arm. He had saddled-up well before daylight to get the mail from the roadside mailbox where an obliging Main Roads driver had left it. We had expected to be camped out for the next ten days.

His horse, Atomic, whom he had been working solidly for weeks objected to the early hour and bucked. He bucked well, going in a tight circle and leaning in so that he almost fell. Edwin was speared out at a tangent and landed heavily on his elbow.

Atomic's treachery in bucking as he did hurt Edwin nearly as much as his injuries.

As well as having broken the bone in his upper arm it was plain to see by the unnatural angle of his elbow that it had been dislocated. Both the arm and elbow swelled rapidly and Edwin was in a great deal of pain. We had only aspirin to give him.

Bill was adjusting Edwin's stirrup-leathers to suit his length of leg and was about to ride to Springvale to get help when Roy appeared.

"No, Bill, don't get on. Ride your own horse. No need to tempt Providence. Ikey broke his leg when I was at Curraghmore last month. I come here and Edwin breaks his arm. I'm darn sure you won't be the third! Here," he handed Bill his own bridle. "Catch your own mare."

Knowing the futility, Bill didn't stop to argue with Roy but put his own saddle on Bangle and galloped her nearly all the way to Springvale.

About halfway he met Archie in his command car, also Springvale bound. Thinking Archie would turn back and take Edwin to town before his arm became too painful, he stopped the vehicle and told Archie what had happened.

It appeared Archie could not turn back. But, if no one was home at Springvale to drive the truck, he would kindly go back to the Main Roads camp to get a driver from there. None of us had ever tried to drive a truck and were hesitant to make an attempt with the Boss away if there was a way out.

There were no drivers at Springvale so Bill and Bangle returned much to our disappointment without the means of getting Edwin to a hospital.

However, while we were steeling ourselves to have a try at truck-driving (the gears were on the knob of the gear lever) Archie had finished his smoko at Springvale and arrived with the

Springvale folk and Geoff the Main Roads driver who had left our mail in the box.

There was nothing much we could do for Edwin but to support his splinted arm in a sling and to give him endless cups of tea and aspirin. Old Sam who had a miner's knowledge of first aid said there was nothing more we could do but as by this time the dislocation was becoming increasingly painful we "borrowed" the Boss's brandy and gave Edwin a generous nip before we put him in beside Geoff in the truck.

Roy was quite upset over the whole business and blamed himself. He had asked if someone could get the mail before we went out but the same question was also asked by Ruth and me. Roy was unlucky. He was a jinx. He was also very emphatic that no one was to ride Atomic — Roy's thoughts ran to a rifle bullet — but taking advantage of everyone talking, Bill and Paddy went up to the yards where Bill rode him. Atomic behaved like a lady's hack.

Roy's theory of accidents happening in threes was sadly confirmed. Hardly had he returned to Curraghmore when a young married man employed to mend a tank on a high stand, fell and broke his neck. The injury was fatal. Roy died the following year.

Roy wanted to get all the gear finished before the races so that he could watch Souvenir in action. He was kept very busy but he managed, while stitching away, to tell us without being hindered by diplomacy, of our saddles. He particularly held in contempt Bill's faithful old battle-scarred saddle and advised throwing it on the rubbish heap.

Mine, with a patch in the flap it had taken me twenty two copper rivets to mend, also came in for much scornful comment. The entire flap with the offending patch was swiftly sliced off and thrown on the growing rubbish pile. The heap was quickly assuming gigantic proportions.

My explanation that I don't usually use rivets to that extent wasn't heard. It was useless arguing with Roy if he didn't feel inclined to debate. He was stone deaf and could interpret conversation only by lip-reading. If he wished to end a conversation or to terminate a losing argument he merely shifted his gaze from his opponent's face back to his work — and that was that.

The big hole had been torn in my saddle-flap when my horse fell backwards down a steep crumbling bank. I jumped — or fell — clear, miraculously landing on my feet. Ranger landed on the broad of his back caught up by a tree, a branch from which had thrust itself under the channel at the back of the saddle and out again through the flap — just about where my knee should have been.

Ranger was a sensible horse though he did have a reputation of kicking eyes out of needles. Luckily again, Stan was with me and he disentangled Ranger while I held his head. No damage, other than that to the saddle flap, was done.

Getting back to the station that night I found we were out of hemp thread to make a wax end to repair the tear. Not being game enough to help myself to the spaying twine I made do with extensive rivetting. It looked a bit startling with all the rivet-heads gleaming in the sunlight and as I didn't want them to scratch the under-flap of the station-owned saddle the rough 'cut' ends of the rivets were uppermost and played havoc with whatever part of me they rubbed against. I was not at all unwilling for Roy to remove that lot.

Roy also objected to my old boots. The soles were parting from the uppers in places and I had them secured with greenhide, but they were comfortable and new boots had to be "broken in."

He also objected to my legging-less state. The others all wore spring-side leggings, even Leo having a cast-off pair of Paddy's but I found them hot. Roy objected on the grounds that he would be in the same camp at the races and I was letting the side down.

"But I don't like leggings, Roy,".

"You should have leggings," he countered.

"They're too hot," I argued knowing I was losing.

He disagreed.

"Oh, right-oh. Make them spring-sides." These could be removed without first taking off boots and spurs.

That didn't please Roy. "Ladies wear pull-ons."

"But I don't want pull-ons."

A scowl was my answer as he repeated that ladies did not wear spring-sides.

"Well," I said, knowing when I was beaten and producing four little nickel horse-shoes, "can I have horse-shoe buckles?"

"Ladies have studs."

I didn't like to ask for bag-leather but apparently ladies are allowed to wear bag-leather leggings. Further conversation would have been wasted anyhow as Roy had turned back to his work.

They did look neat when Roy finished them. He stained them a deep mahogany and the brass studs looked very businesslike. I wore them at the races one day to please Roy and as the Boss was very vocal in his admiration of them I later gave them to him. He still wears them and they suit him very well.

# 12.

# OFF TO THE RACES AGAIN

The Laura Races passed off much the same as they did in other years, only this time we had Souvenir and Simplifier, the Boss's gun horse and kept them right up until race-day. As both had raced before they had nothing to learn about the ways of racetracks so we got them into condition along the roads, Ruth riding Simplifier and I the mare.

At the race meeting itself, Ruth and I presided over the tea stall. It was an innovation as previously there had been liquid refreshments offering at the bar only.

We robbed the public so successfully with our teas and our raffles that the race club profited by £70 nett ($140). On the strength of that effort the club presented us, later and by registered post, with the handsome gold brooches of Life Members. Though very flattered and proud of the honour we felt that the paying public should have shared it with us.

The money was put in a fund to start building an open-air dance hall. Until then the dances had been held in the front room of the pub which was small and a little uneven, to put it mildly, in the flooring. Also it was separated only by an open doorway from the bar and the men found it all too easy to disappear, often beyond recall, after each dance.

Bill and I decided against going into Cooktown for the races there even if given the opportunity, for Bill was to break-in some young horses. Ruth and the Boss were away at some other festivity but were returning in time to train the Cooktown horses for the meeting. The arrangement was that horses accepted as grassfed for the Laura meet could start at Cooktown without having to be paddocked at Cooktown prior to their meeting.

Edwin was still away nursing his arm. Souvenir, with some of the other Laura horses, had gone down the long seventy-mile trek to Cooktown and was reported to be looking even fitter than at Laura. I had my fingers crossed that she'd win in Cooktown, too.

Bill and I had just come in one evening from bringing in a mob of young things for Bill to start work on. We had sorted them out into handy holding paddocks ready to begin in the morning and were just sitting down to a very late meal when we thought we heard a truck coming.

Ruth had sent Miles's partner, Ian — also doubling as the Boss's jockey — to get us so as Ian had come over fifty rough miles to take us to the races we hastily packed a few clothes and rolled our swags while Ian consumed the last of the coffee, and left.

Ruth had booked a room for us at the hotel but as we reached our destination at two a.m., two days before the races, we lacked the audacity to disturb the over-worked publican and unrolled our swags on the cement slab under the mango tree at the foot of the back steps.

There we slept soundly until the licensee coming down to light the big range for breakfast, nearly tripped over our legs and offered us a cup of tea.

The races were notable for a near-brawl. It was almost civil war as most of the population of town and hinterland were involved. The central figure was Souvenir — the Curraghmore mare.

We had heard that a rival faction — henceforth referred to as "They" — were intending to protest "if the mare won". The grounds for the protest were to be that she had been fed other than grass during the days before the meeting.

I couldn't see how they were going to do it, for even supposing she had been fed — which as far as I know and believe, she wasn't — she had been accepted and had raced as grassfed in Laura and was consequently eligible to race in Cooktown.

Also I couldn't see why "They" should protest only if she won. Surely, if she were cornfed, being beaten out of first place wouldn't automatically make her into a true grass-eater.

It seemed too silly and trivial to worry about so no one did until the mare won and "They" protested.

The jockeys were bustled unceremoniously from the galvanised-iron hot-box that served as their changing-room and the officials and witnesses moved in. The inquiry was under way.

The jockeys lined up along the outside walls like extra-colourful but rather straggly hollyhocks straining to pick up what they could of the "proceedings". Such information they did hear was readily passed on to the crowd.

"They" had a formidable lot of witnesses. None of them were members of the usual Cooktown racing fraternity and seemed to be prepared to swear to anything.

The usually meek and mild Miles Morris was the hero of the day. He let the rival witnesses get more and more eloquent and more and more confident as they told their tale of bringing the mare back to the Peninsula from a training establishment in Mareeba and that they had fed her all the way over.

Perhaps they thought the real drover would have been half-way down the Peninsula with another mob and wouldn't know the difference. In any case it was a ridiculous statement.

Miles was really stirred. It was a threat to his integrity.

"YOUR plant took delivery of the mare?" he queried lining his slightly built horseman's frame up to face the burly opposition. "MY plant took delivery of that mare and she was NOT fed on the road over. Anyhow, how would you know what happened? You left your plant in Mareeba and got a lift back with a Main Roads truck!"

Righteously indignant, Miles sat down on the only lager case not occupied by the committee. The opposition, deflated, decided on silence and the protest was dismissed.

Though the matter closed with the opposition's principals at the dismissal of the protest, their understrappers who had been putting in time at the bar tried to provoke a few fights. They had backed the second horse quite heavily.

The drover who was prepared to swear to taking delivery of the mare and feeding her, a strongly built fellow in his late twenties, was telling anyone who would listen what he was going to do to the Boss, a veritable Hercules of about five and a half feet in height and weighing all of eight stone. As well as that, he was more than twice as old as his would-be opponent.

Bill and his mates and also the Boss's younger mates were all willing to step in and fight his fights for him if necessary. His two biggest and most aggressive friends insisted on escorting him everywhere he went much to his intense irritation. He looked like a cranky little bantam rooster who couldn't get through the wire to fight.

At last the indignity of his situation got the better of him and he turned on his self-appointed body-guard.

"They'll think a man's a bloody dingo!" he complained and getting free of them walked up and down the footpath outside the bar where his would-be "murderer" was drinking. Ten minutes later, self-respect restored and honour satisfied, he retired to bed. The fighting man never lifted his eyes from his beer.

Miles was due to be slaughtered too and it upset his calculations. He had sandwiched the races into a very tightly-planned schedule in which he was to leave Maitland to muster the morning after the races. He had counted on leaving town that night.

His truck was loaded-up ready to go, native stockboys in the shadows waiting to climb aboard and leave but he stayed until the next day idly making the time spin out so that no one would think he was running from a fight.

Souvenir couldn't care less and continued to keep her corn-fed look to spite them. A year later, after her foal was born, she left the station with the drovers, heading for Curraghmore with her foal at foot and as sleek and as shiny as ever.

# 13.

# THE HARDER THEY FALL

The horse sports which interested Bill and me even more than the races which had gone before, were full of excitement. Unfortunately Bill provided a lot of the excitement.

The news of his Mareeba win had travelled to Cooktown and to fill in time between events the announcer was enlarging in the strain of "local boy makes good" on his win.

Bill always considered Cooktown sports ground to be unlucky for him. He had been thrown more often in the rodeo events than he had ridden "time" and he had never had a win there. This trip was no exception.

As he came out on his first mount in the buck-jump, the commentator had barely begun on the saga of Bill's Mareeba prowess when the Mareeba champ bit the dust. That was only for starters. He barely left the chutes in the bullock-ride and he was on foot again.

It wasn't his day. There were only the sporting events left, the flag, bending, figure-eight and other equine gymnastics. Ruth and I had both been lent horses for these events and Ruth had won most of the ladies' classes. We didn't realise Bill didn't have a mount for the men's events and re-lent ours to someone else.

Uncle Bill the drover, the Boss's brother, had a horse Bill could borrow. It was one he had just brought back in his droving plant from Mareeba, looked a reasonable sort of horse and was in good condition.

"Quiet," said old Billy before anyone asked, "he's a corker little horse, like. He's a lady's hack."

Knowing old Billy, Bill first rode the horse in a round yard in the area inside the race-track. Surprisingly, he did behave like a lady's hack. Bill cantered him around to warm him up and he seemed quite O.K.

Came the first flag in the flag race and the grey horse showed no inclination to turn. He wanted to keep going straight ahead. Bill touched him on the shoulder with a spur to try to make him turn. The effect was sudden and startling. The grey took off in a series of nasty bucks and bolted. In its flight it came to a deep drain and propped suddenly before it hurdled it and galloped off. Unfortunately the borrowed stirrup leather broke as the horse propped and Bill landed in the gutter.

One of his mates set off after the runaway to stop it leaving the racecourse and going "bush" with the saddle but the moment he put spurs to his horse's sides it began pig-jumping too, and careered about the course in the opposite direction, much to the delight of the crowd.

Loath to be out of the excitement, a host of other horsemen joined the fray and the two horses and one rider were soon returned to the fold.

Bill's day was not over. Ruth and I were listening with interest to some tall stories being presented as Gospel truths by an old hand to a group of tourists from the passenger ship "Elsanna" when someone yelled — "He's caught in the stirrup!"

We looked around quickly to see that "he" was my young husband. He and Ruth's beau had mounted double-bank preparatory to a Gretna Green event when Bill's run-away "bride" slapped the horse down the flanks with his open hands to enliven the proceedings.

It had the desired effect; the horse ducked its head and began to pig-jump. The instigator of the action promptly came off and clutching Bill for support as he was leaving, pulled him down too.

All would have been well if Bill's foot hadn't gone through the stirrup iron and stuck there. I had a few, very frightened seconds as Bill hung head-down while the horse's hoofs bucked around his trailing head and body. It seemed impossible that he could miss being trampled. Then, his boot came off, his foot slipped out and he jumped up unhurt.

I breathed again. That has been his last rodeo.

After the races we began our equivalent of house-hunting. We were looking for somewhere our cattle and horses could be grazed and which would provide a roof over our heads as well. Uncle Bill was enthusiastic about us joining him at Bald Hills, a small run outside Cooktown which he used as a depot for his droving horses and where he was also trying to breed a few "corker" foals.

Old Billy Wallace had been droving from the Coen end to Mareeba for many years and was well known and well liked all along the drover's road. No matter how hard the trip he could always raise a chuckle at some funny incident that happened — often to himself.

After we went out to Bald Hills and he was well in his sixties he wrote us a letter. Part of it read, "I suppose you heard I got married. I just couldn't stay single any longer."

Fortunately, Bill's bride, Sadie, also liked horses and the bush and went droving with old Billy until the day he died suddenly in the camp with her on their way to pick up another big mob.

Bald Hills was coastal country and not at all like Bill's drier forest country. Bill decided against the move as soon as he saw the tangle of undergrowth fringing the small house clearing.

"The little poddies (from the Tableland) would get lost".

And so we came back, still homeless.

We had written to all the Crown Land Agents in the Far North inquiring about vacant crown leases but the only piece vacant came back with the attached note, "Don't touch it, lady. It's desert."

An old hand from the Coen was reported to be wanting to

sell. We wrote to him. He replied that though he didn't want to sell outright he was interested in making a deal with us. Could we meet him?

Though we understood his reluctance to sever all ties with the bush, Bill read as far as the "deal" and that was that. He had been given enough deals to last him for some time. A few years later Hardy bought the same property.

I don't quite know how it came about, seeing we had come to town with Ian in the truck, but Bill and I together with Bennie from Springvale brought the race-horses back home again. There were only a few of them so we travelled along quite smartly. Before we came to the East Normanby and after we had climbed up from the coastal plain by way of the Grecian Bend and the not so Gentle Annie, we came to the line of posts, mostly burnt, that was once the boundary fence of Harvest Home. Bennie passed the remark that he had once tried to buy the two thousand acre block from Bill's father so that he could run a few head of his own there while working on adjoining Springvale.

Harvest Home had been taken-up originally in the eighteen eighties as an agricultural farm though I doubt if much farming was carried on there. A big home had been built, four large rooms surrounded by a wide verandah and with a separate kitchen block. The doors were of Cooktown cedar but the rest of the house was pit-sawn on the spot. Floorboards of beautiful white Leichhardt planks were used throughout. The site of the saw-pit could be recognised from a man-made "hole" along the creek and a rusty pit-saw was later unearthed from a rubbish dump.

For some reason, Bill's father bought Harvest Home in Bill's name. He had removed the buildings to be re-erected at either Butcher Hill or Lakefield leaving the kitchen standing as a camp for travellers. Unfortunately the latter was burnt.

The men's hut at Butcher Hill was constructed of the pit-sawn slabs, "dropped" into place, one above the other and held in place by uprights. Ripple iron, a very finely corrugated sheet, was also used from the old building and the floor was of the dressed Leichhardt.

The main building went to Lakefield. A large cedar bookcase full of both English and Australian books from the late nineteenth century was given to the Cooktown hospital. Horses and cattle were taken to Butcher Hill and all that remained now were a few fruit trees on the river and creek, a private cemetery and the burnt posts and tangled wire.

I do not know whether Bill had made his mind up previously or if Bennie had suggested it with his remark but when we reached home Bill asked the Boss about our going there to live.

His father didn't think much of the idea, suggesting that we would be better off if Bill took a job that was offering to run the camp on one of the big stations further North, but we wanted something of our own.

We wanted the chance to try to breed good cattle too and to try our wings. The time had come for the parting of the ways so, for the price of some Council rates that were owing, we were free to do as we liked at Harvest Home.

# 14.

# THE PARTING OF THE WAYS

Bill arranged to stay on at Butcher Hill for the next muster, dipping, and then we were to go over to the other side while he underwent the operation postponed from his previous visit. The day Bill went into hospital, my mother who had come down from the station with us, caught the 'plane bound for the south and civilisation.

Bill was a very impatient patient. As he had to spend the first two weeks of his hospital sentence flat on his back, not even being allowed to sit, the time dragged horribly and he was heartily weary of town.

As luck would have it, Hardy and Iris came in from Mt. Garnet just as Bill was released so we went back with them for a short stay. Hardy didn't approve of us going to Harvest Home either.

According to him, the Peninsula was "no good", freight costs were too high and the cost of making improvements almost double that prevailing in the Garnet area. The pasture grasses, even counting the Townsville "lucerne" were inferior and there was the annual long "Dry" season. There were manager's jobs offering in the Garnet. We would be better putting in for one of them.

Probably there was a lot of truth in what Hardy said but like true Peninsula pikers we refused to be tempted from the safety of our home scrubs.

Thereupon, Hardy decided that seeing we had made up our minds to stay in the Peninsula, he had better see that we did it in style.

Other than some saddle horses and a packhorse (complete with packs) we had no means of locomotion. The solution to that was to buy a truck and Hardy would sell us one.

We protested we didn't have the money to buy a truck but Hardy dismissed that with a wave of his hand and generously sold us an old ex-Army Ford that he and a mate used to take their racehorses from meet to meet. The partner wasn't consulted until after the deed was done.

Later, we couldn't see how we had ever hoped to manage without a truck. Also, I think Hardy regretted his rash generosity but he didn't reneg and the old Ford served us faithfully for many years.

Now that we were truck-owners, it took no time at all to fill all the available truck-space with things to take home. It is really remarkable all the things that have to be bought when there is nothing besides a few hobble-chains, a set of billycans and a pannikin or two and some kitchen utensils, in kitty.

Hardy, Iris and Iris's mother came to our rescue and raided their own stocks and the local stores for oddments for us. Bill's mother did a little petty pilfering from the farm's extensive toolery on our account.

With a thousand gallon (5000 litre) tank, a set of concrete wash tubs and a cooking stove, several cases of kerosene — especially bought in four gallon tins, two to a wooden case instead of by the forty-four gallon drum so that we'd have both buckets and furniture — three chairs (from the farm), a double bed (Iris's mother's) and six months' stores stowed in the tank, we were well-loaded!

As neither of us had learnt to drive and as Hardy didn't consider the new Mulligan Highway an ideal place for learners, he decided to come with us. Iris's father, Bill's mother and I were to follow in Hardy's utility.

We were scheduled to leave at daylight, but Hardy, impatient to be gone, had us out of bed much earlier and supervised the last-minute packing of goods with a critical eye. A handy little white table Iris's mother had given us was rejected as "useless in the bush". Iris was sneaking her old folding bassinet, on loan to us, into a narrow space when Hardy spotted it remarking on the foolishness of people who had babies "in the bush".

One of Hardy and Iris's babies was to be born literally "in the bush" a hundred miles to the north-west of Coen. Arthur Wallace suggested the baby girl be called "Merle Una" as a permanent reminder of her birth place but Iris said she didn't need any reminders and called her daughter Beth.

Our stove had come complete with a protective sack-bag stuffed with grass which we all gathered was for it to sit on to cushion it against the shocks ahead but as Hardy was the only able-bodied person there, he had the loading of the stove in his province. It went right at the tail-end with the precious cases of kerosene, its grass pillow hurled over its offending head and a box of flower-cuttings hurled over our own.

We were packed. With a whirlwind "Goodbye" to Iris, Hardy was behind the wheel and we, not daring to delay, were away.

Hardy had the Ford bowling along the Mulligan Highway in fine style pointing out its finer points to Bill as they went.

Bill's mother who was going back to Butcher Hill with us and whose suggestion it was to invest in tinned kero, watched frustrated and furious as the kerosene cases bounded, bounced and bashed into each other at every bump. The stove, too, just in from the tailboard, did a bit of what I now recognise as advanced Rock'n Roll as it weathered the stones and gutters in the road.

Needless to say, when we pulled up for lunch, it was evident from the kerosene trail we were leaving that we had one unpunctured tin out of six. The cases had shattered and their loosed nails had done their worst. Worse was to follow. On reading the invoice we found that instead of being cheap furniture the cases were dear firewood at three and six (35c) each.

Half-way along I joined Bill and Hardy in the lead but not until we had eaten lunch on the bleakest, most desert-stricken spot on the road — the Short Cut over the Desailly Range. The road followed the flat country around, skirting the steep grades of the range, but a tentative start had been made on what is now the main road over the range.

In those days it was a major achievement for a command car to traverse it. That we had come over it, loaded as we were, forever sealed the truck's reputation as a "puller".

A slight mishap kept us stranded on that cliff-faced ridge for lunch. The gears slipped out as we were going up the longest, steepest grade. Fortunately, Hardy has mechanical ability and we were soon on our way. Equally fortunately, for we have no mechanical ability, it has never happened since.

The Highway at that time might have been "high" as far as the hills and ridges went but it didn't mean that the free space above the truck was by any means high. Low limbs criss-crossed the road every few miles and had to be carefully negotiated.

Besides having the tank on board, we also had the equally precious — to me at least — double-bed. It reclined awkwardly, packed by Hardy, along one of its longer sides, pointing its rather angular hip-bones and unattached legs to the trees above. Its height made progress much slower than Hardy would have liked.

Within sight of the Maitland turn-off, a chance limb hit the bed, knocked the headboard soaring into space and split the four boards that formed the frame.

The rear-guard picked up the head-board minus one leg. It had gone much further afield and some months later one of Miles's boys found it while out mustering and it was duly returned to its three companions minus only the castor from its base. In the meantime we slept with the foot of the bed supported by the off-cuts from the shed's posts.

Due to the lunchtime delay, we reached the Byerstown

Range just on dark, which was unfortunate in that Hardy, in an energetic burst of re-wiring hadn't got around to doing the lights although he had stripped them of the old wiring.

The foot-brake, working overtime on the road behind, had also gone on strike. Suffice it to say we finally, very thankfully, reached the bottom and Butcher Hill just before midnight.

Bill had to go to town to re-new his revolver licence so Hardy decided he would show his father-in-law the sights and take Bill to Cooktown.

There were no bridges over the Normanbys then, just bridge-gangs camped hopefully on the banks. Each Wet their carefully erected piles would be washed downstream but eventually they did get bridges across both rivers.

Most of the time however, although the bridges were there in case of flood, the approaches would wash-out so that the bridges appeared as islands inaccessible in the swirling waters.

Archie was still Boss of the road-gang and Hardy with his passengers and another station truck as travelling companion, met him on the bank of the Big Normanby. The crossing, going straight across from where the road entered the water was waist-deep. The men got out and joined Archie surveying the waters. Archie wanted to get across to the town side of the river.

The station ringers who, by way of their occupation, had reason to know all the shallow crossings, told Archie of a better crossing, diagonally across, just upstream from the one he was considering.

"The water here is waist-deep," said Hardy who was not one to avoid necessary risks but knowing this was an unnecessary one.

"That's nothing," returned Archie, not to be outdone. "MY command car has gone through water up to HERE!" He indicated with his hand a spot just under his top shirt button.

"Righto," said the ringers game for anything in Archie's vehicle. "We'll go over with you."

All hands sprang aboard but when Archie sank out of sight as the current took the car downstream a trifle, all hands — save Archie who could not and Bill who was too polite — left the sinking ship and struck out for dry land, there to laugh themselves into near-convulsions.

Once settled in the deepest hole, the command car rested like a rock. It being a left-hand drive vehicle Archie was on the downstream side and all his packages, mail and parcels sailed merrily past from their unsafe positions on the seat beside him and from the open-fronted glove-box.

Bill and Archie dived frantically trying to retrieve them as the current bore them away but when Archie reached out to grab some important Main Roads mail and his own unsecured rubber-cushion launched itself into the stream, they gave up and waded out.

One drum of kerosene and much of Archie's good humour went down with the waters. The former was never recovered.

Wally, Iris's father who enjoyed life and a good joke, had never enjoyed himself more. He sat on the creek bank (he had laughed so much he could not stand) and laughed until the tears came to his eyes.

"It was worth six trips up that road, breakdown and all, to see," he recounted to us even then wiping tears from his eyes and struggling for composure. "The way she just sank out of sight and those two silly bees grabbing at everything that floated past."

The tale improved with each telling but he usually had to give it best when he got to the bit about "MY command car can go through water up to HERE." Archie's Waterhole like many Follies, Mistakes and Catastrophies lives on in local legend.

Nevertheless, as Bill's driving experience was limited to three very short jaunts around the house-square at Butcher Hill, I didn't laugh too much in case the name was changed after we crossed to "Billy's Disaster".

Bill scorned such subversive thought and though he had failed to locate top gear but would shoot into reverse instead, he was confident he'd learn along the way and so we set out along the boggy trail early the next morning bound for Home Sweet

Home.

Once out on the Main Road Bill soon found top gear and we went along in fine style, thinking how fortunate we were to be going to a place of our own at last. Except for our horses, a few head of cattle, Growler and her five baby pups, my hen and nine chicks and our non-essential wedding gifts, all our worldly possessions were on that truck. We felt pretty good.

The Normanby proved no worry. Another truck — one that had witnessed Archie's disgrace — reached the river just behind us and offered to take our truck across. I accepted quickly but I think Bill would have liked to try to negotiate it under his own steam. The Little Normanby was no trouble either and we sailed blithely to the turn-off that led to our new home.

While Bill concentrated on negotiating bumps and gullies, I was indulging in day-dreams all with the same theme — we're on our own at last.

Suddenly the dreams ended. The truck stopped. There we were in the middle of a steep gully. The sides went straight up in front of us and the truck's nose went straight down. There was nothing else to do but to get out and survey the damage.

The axe could not be found to cut rails to fill the void. It turned up later inside the tank where it had cut through a bag of flour, some sugar and a packet of sago, mercifully sparing the tank itself. Stones were unobligingly hard to find. With nothing more constructive to do, we surveyed the damage again until we became aware of a truck approaching. Ruth and Miles to the rescue!

Miles also had as cargo Growler and her quins, the latter safely enclosed in an old tin hanging meat-safe on loan from Butcher Hill. It proved an unfortunate choice for a dog kennel and I had a difficult time trying to evict them later. Growler and the pups could be discounted as helpers and by the look on Ruth's face she and Miles had been arguing again — probably about horses — so she could be counted out as well. But Miles himself loomed as a larger-than-life Sir Galahad.

With the exception of Ruth and the pups (Growler stood on

her little hind legs and poked her nose in too) we all looked inside the upraised bonnet hoping for inspiration. The coil — I'll take Miles' word that it was a coil — was behaving queerly. It was bubbling and surging like a small thermal mud-spring.

While we leaned over, heads pressed together and Growler whimpering to be lifted up for a better view, even Miles was spell-bound by its action. We watched bewitched by its contortions and not knowing what to do as with a loud hiss it melted completely and departed its life as a useful truck component in a dashing spurt like a geyser.

Shocked and horrified we replaced the bonnet gently securing it with a piece of greenhide and decided Bill and Miles would go back to the Main Roads camp for more specialised technical advice.

With Miles gone, Ruth became more talkative.

"Harvest Home is just over that ridge," she said. "Let's walk."

We walked. Harvest Home wasn't all that far away but Ruth had her ridges mixed. We had to pass that one, and another and then another one and it was awfully hot and steamy.

The site of our new home wasn't exactly awe-inspiring either. All that was left of the black-bean, cedar and Leichhardt home was a few derelict house stumps, a clump or two of bravely-flowering purple granny-caps, some sheets of crumpled iron and a pile of empty tins. Plus a five foot high growth of turpentine grass.

We saw all we wanted to see in the first ten seconds. Ruth found a sheet of iron approximating her size and flopped onto it in the half-hearted shade of the one tree. I found two pieces to accommodate my spreading perimeter and after they had cooled a little, joined her.

I woke first and headed for the creek looking for water to be stopped by a cry from Ruth as she tried to find me in the long grass. We went to the creek which was a little cooler and regretted we hadn't brought the tucker box with us. We needn't have worried as Miles and Bill had already reached the creek and while

Miles was collecting fire-wood Bill was coming to look for us.

I expect they wished we would have stayed at the truck for there was water in the gully there but it was nice to boil the billy with water from our own creek and sit on our own ground even if the old fence line said we were still five or six feet off the boundary.

Back again to the truck, on foot of course as Miles couldn't get his truck around the Ford and there were no spare coils at the camp. There was nothing for it but to climb into Miles's truck and head for town.

Head for town was right as we didn't get there. A few hundred yards along the main road from our turn-off a cloud must have burst on top of us. The water ran across the road about a foot deep and within minutes the gullies were awash as water rushed down them in white-capped waves.

Miles reversed while the going was still good and we retreated to the Main Roads camp. There good news awaited us. An owner-driver with a Ford similar to ours was sheltering there too and he had a spare coil. Half a mile the other side of the camp we could hear another truck roaring as, bogged to the axles on the Mulligan Highway, it tried desperately to get free. Some time later the roaring stopped and that truck's occupants came into camp with a big diesel truck that had got across the spongy place before it caved in.

We sat around the fire drinking the road gang's tea while the Ford driver located a used, but functional, coil. He and the other driver came back with us later and the second man put his experienced head under the bonnet for a second or two and withdrew it to tell us we were lucky to get as far as we did. During Hardy's re-wiring, a two volt resistor had been left disconnected and six volts had been going through a four volt coil. To make matters worse, when the truck stalled, we had both forgotten to turn off the ignition. Small wonder the melting coil issued forth like Old Faithful!

Two of the road-men chivalrously gave up their bunks to Ruth and me. I sank gratefully on to mine and went to sleep immediately. Ruth and the Ford man stayed up half the night playing hill-billies on a scratchy old gramophone but I didn't notice the scratches and squeaks until next morning.

Daylight dawned on a sunlit world. Although it hadn't been a Friday, yesterday had been the thirteenth. With a bit of luck the fourteenth would see us home. It did.

Quite a convoy pulled out from the camp. The bogged truck was rescued after a lot of pulling with patent pulleys, manpower and lastly, as the road dried out a little, by the big diesel.

The road was like a nearly-set jelly. It looked solid enough but just walking on it made it quake. Ruth and I amused ourselves by jumping on it to create small earth-tremors until the truck was extricated and on its way and Miles could get around it to go back to our truck. The previous night the men had towed it back out of the gully so it had not, as I had feared, been washed away.

With the new coil and the wiring adjusted it was a simple matter to cross the gully. Miles and Ruth, friends once more, followed.

The bare hilltop didn't offer much encouragement for home-building but we unloaded both trucks while the released pups scampered about getting in the road of everyone. Once the axe was discovered in its hideout, poles were cut for our tents — or rather, our two borrowed flies. Being flies, they had to be slung very low as this was the storm season and to get any amount of "wall" into them at all, the ridge pole was hung so low that we had to stoop everywhere else but directly under it.

An old round table, gift from Bill's mother and relic of "old" Harvest Home took up the tucker tent and the broken bed-frame occupied the second fly to the exclusion of just about anything else.

The pups, annoyed at being ousted from the meat-safe, took over the cooler space underneath the bed-spring. I never became used to them and when I'd flop down on the bed to rest, I'd bound up again smartly as five pups protested loudly against my weighty invasion of their territory.

The tent-flies gave us two rooms, the "bedroom" and the

"dining-room". The stove stood outside in an open-air kitchen with a sheet of galvanised iron propped against it to be used as a "roof" in time of rain.

Water had to be carted by billycan from the creek so we didn't use any more of it than we could help. The "bathroom" with hot or cold, depending on the weather, was a rock-hole in the creek.

Ruth and Miles collaborated on the putting-together of the stove. There was a piece left-over that no one could identify but it mustn't have been important as the stove functioned without it. They were quite proud of their achievement and we celebrated with a cup of tea boiled on the stove.

Miles, as usual, was in a hurry to get back so they couldn't stay any longer. Grateful for their help we walked down to the creek to see them off and then walked slowly back up the hill to finish the tea still left in the pot.

We were on our own.

# 15.

# NEW SHOOTS ON THE FAMILY TREE

Despite the terrific heat and the very occasional downpour of rain which soaked everything and everyone, it was fun settling in. Norman, with our new neighbours, Jock and Gladys Christensen, came over to give us a hand to lay-out and build the shed where we were to live. It was a large building fifty by thirty feet, with a wall at the western end and a stove recess jutting out from the middle of one long side.

We moved from the tents just as soon as we could, camping in one section of the shed until the rest was built. Round bush timber was used with sawn-timber battens to which the iron was nailed. Some of the iron had come from the old convent at Cooktown. It had been the "fence" and the top of the sheets had been cut into sharp peaks to discourage intruders.

The truck moved in with us, too, to get out of the wet, though Ruth remarked it was the first time she had ever seen a truck in a kitchen.

There was an unexpected delay in carpentering when a cattle buyer rode in looking for Jock. Though the buyer had his plant and droving boys with him, the whole business was a total surprise to Jock and Gladys but after a few words of explanation and a drink of tea, Jock decided to get the cattle the buyer, a Cairns butcher, required.

The forced builder's labourers downed tools smartly and became ringers again for two days. Then the buyer left happily behind almost a hundred head of prime fats to take them by way of the China Camp track to Mossman and then Cairns.

Reluctantly, the men went back to the job. The roof was completed and the one wall put up. The bed-spring was supported at its head-end on the bottom rail wall-plate and propped on two sawn-off house stumps at the other. The foot was on a slightly lower level than the head so that, on awakening each morning, our feet and legs from the knees down were usually dangling.

The floor, of course, was dirt. Water was carted, first by camp billycan, then by bucket (per kind favour of Norman) and then in a forty-four gallon drum Jock lent us until our rainwater tank filled.

When you start from "scratch" in the middle of nowhere things that would be considered rubbish elsewhere are often treasured.

I optimistically planted out scores of plants, cuttings and seedlings. A very rare few survived the perils of infancy. Storms began to fall, some good, heavy downpours and some all noise, wind and no rain. The road was fast dissolving into mud and unrecognisable nothingness.

At Butcher Hill, Bill's mother was constantly writing me notes and urging Bill, who seemed to be up there most of the time, to "Get Lennie into town." But Christmas saw us still there — at Kings Plains for the day with Bill riding down from Butcher Hill to be with us for twenty-four hours, returning to Butcher Hill the next day.

Then the Kings Plains folk began to get uneasy. I was forbidden to pull weeds, to reach up for things, to bend down (rather difficult) or to do anything at all energetic. All these things are liable to choke babies with their own birthcord apparently. Another neighbour calling when I was carrying a bucket of water told me to carry a bucket in each hand — to "even the strain" — or none at all. I was learning pre-natal care as I went.

I reached my friend's house in Cooktown in plenty of time

though Bill did get bogged and have to walk on his way home. Young John took his time. He arrived just after I had seen Ruth off on the 'plane that was to take her to a job on an Arabian stud farm in Victoria.

To be exact, he made his arrival at 5am 20th January 1953.

I thought that once the baby was born, my troubles would be over. They had just begun. They began with the coming of the Wet. I could not get home! The people who were so keen to get me into town seemed to have no inclination to get me out!

It rained and rained with aggravating monotony. Bill, I gathered from scrappy little notes that filtered through per courtesy of the Main Roads, was mustering with Miles. A couple of fine breaks came, lasted two days and dissipated into more rain.

Bill and Miles continued to muster despite the rain. No one would take a homesick mother and babe out on that road, let alone a precious truck. It became unequivocally clear that it is one thing to get an expectant mother who could prove an embarrassment into town but another to get a mother and child out again.

Joyce and I struggled with wet nappies and a cranky baby while the new mother got crankier every day as the proud father failed to make an appearance. Finally, in the baby's third week, I was urgently summoned one evening to a shop across the street.

"Helenvale wants you on the 'phone", said Dee handing me the instrument.

A very clear "Hullo, that you, Lennie?" came over the wires. Then something that could have been the Icelandic National Anthem or the Martian Philharmonic Orchestra took over. I couldn't understand a word. Also, I don't like 'phones in electrical storms and this one crackled and hissed as I held it well away and called Dee.

She rang the handle vigorously, punched the side of the instrument and kicked the wall. She carried on quite a satisfactory conversation after this treatment and handed the 'phone back to me saying, "Bill's on the line."

We exchanged terse sweet-nothings for a short while at the top of our voices while the Martian/Icelandic theme kept on.

"Can you come out?" shouted Bill.

"Yes. I'll see Bluey in the morning. He took the Land Rover to Starcke."

The 'phone lapsed into gibberish so I handed it back to Dee who joggled and banged once more.

I tried again. "I'll see Bluey when he gets in tonight and get him to run me out in the morning." Bluey had the town's only four wheel drive, one of a total of eight vehicles for the town.

Bill's reply came loud and clear. "Come tonight, mate. Might be set-in tomorrow."

I turned to Dee. "Now? He wants me to go now!" To Bill, "Righto, be seeing you."

I ran across the road to tell Joyce.

"Now?" she echoed. "But Bluey isn't back yet. The road is all washed-out to Helenvale." She pushed back a wisp of her blonde hair a trick she had when worrying about something. "I'll get Norm."

Norm came out, as usual with advice and offers of help.

"If Bill wants you to go now, you had better go. If the weather sets in it might be another couple of months before you get another chance."

"Oh no!" I shuddered at the thought.

"It's seven now," Norm resumed calmly. "Joyce and I have had tea. You have yours and Joyce can pack. I'll get the truck ready."

"Gee, Norm! Thanks!" was all I could think to say.

I tried to eat but didn't succeed. Wet nappies were wrapped in plastic and soiled ones soaking in the boiler for the happy morrow, were retrieved and wrapped in more plastic. (What did people do before the invention of plastic?)

Grabbing the numerous suitcases required for five weeks in town — before and after baby — mosquito nets and blankets fresh

Loaded pack horses at the Laura Store, 1950's.

The late Ruth Shephard breaking-in.

Jim Callaghan of Palmerville boils the billy at Laura races.

Gostelow's Urge Lass wins the Coen Bracelet from Bill Shephard's Rajah.

Bill Wallace, the typical Peninsula drover and "ringer".

from the mail, the baby's tin bath and, last but not least, the baby, we left with goodbyes to Joyce, in Norm's truck.

"Watch out for fumes," cautioned Norm making a blind gesture towards the floor on my side where what should have been going out in the exhaust was seeping through at my feet. "Keep the baby's head up near the window."

Fumes were the least of our worries; we reached Helenvale at 10.10pm. The first twenty miles were behind us and poor, kind Norm had to go back.

Young John had the best sleep he'd had for many nights so if it were due to the fumes, I can feel nothing but gratitude to them.

At the pub, Mrs Leary, mother of our other Norman, was waiting with tea and advice backed up by her own experience. Norman wasn't home but he was to appear in the morning to take Johnnie and me as far as he could in his truck.

Bill and I found plenty to talk about until just before daylight when it was time to go. Bill went ahead with the horses and empty pack-saddles while Norman, myself, Johnnie and a mate of Norman's came behind with the filled pack-bags in the truck. Bill waited at each eroded gully — horses being easily as fast as motor trucks — made sure we negotiated it safely and then went on to the next one.

Norman had lent me a long-sleeved shirt and a pair of riding trousers as I hadn't anticipated riding home. I never went anywhere without my big ten gallon hat.

A couple of times I thought the truck could go no further but thanks to the combined efforts of the three men, we continued. At last we came to a creek that stopped us. We said "Goodbye and thanks" to Norman and Jack and neither party wasted time getting away in case more rain came.

Bill carried young John, the latter clad in a slippery coating of olive oil as protection against the sun and suspended in a sheeting sling of sorts from Bill's shoulder. We must have had the sling all wrong, for, though assured by the old-timers it was the best way to carry a baby, it did not work well for us. Bill carried the slipping little thing in the crook of one arm till that arm ached and then he changed arms.

Three years later, Ruth and her husband carried their first-born home in a cardboard carton on the front of the pommel with a piece of the ever useful plastic stretched across the top to shield the baby from showers. That is by far the best way. Gladys used a variation of it to carry her boy home. She used a butcher's basket and when he could sit up, carried him stark-naked sitting on a cushion in front of her while she held an umbrella over them both! Only quiet horses can be used for this.

There were no storms the day we rode out — just the soul-searing heat that preceeds a violent tropical downpour. Bill cursed the horses. They were too slow. For myself, I had no complaints, I had Bill; I had the little fellow and I was headed for home.

"If I only had Hawk or Nancy," was Bill's continual complaint. "We could canter along a bit. These old things can't even walk without stumbling."

Sometimes the packhorses, with Johnnie's handsome blue tin bath high aloft on Maureen, walked into a patch of bog and plunged around in it getting further and further from the road. Bill was not at all pleased with the situation. Oh, to be single again!

As we came to one creek he signalled to stop.

"Little fellow's getting overheated," said the conscientious drover, so we pulled up. While Bill set the eatables out on the tucker cover, I doused our oily, red son in the running water and left him on a napkin on another pack cover to dry.

There was barely time to feed ourselves and John when Bill, with an eye on a low, black cloud-front, began packing-up.

"Come on," he urged. "The storm will beat us if you don't hurry!"

I hurried. Travelling along at a very slow walk in the heat, we barely reached home as in swept the leaf-laden wind that heralded the storm. Taking Johnnie, I ran inside to shelter while Bill attended to the horses.

There was a day to dry the nappies and we were off again, leaving early to beat the rain, but late enough to let the rivers run down a little after the previous night's rain.

Both Normanbys were high. The East, a narrow, swift-running stream in flood was a "bit of a dip" in the middle so that we had to cross bare-back carrying our saddles on our shoulders so that they would not get wet as the horses dipped under water when they lost their foot-hold momentarily mid-stream.

Bill went across first to test the crossing and returned for his saddle. Next we both came across, he with John and I with my saddle and lastly, for the water was too deep for the packs, Bill brought the packs across in a "boat" he contrived from a berkmyre cover. Re-mounting, Johnnie and I kept an eye on the horses until Bill packed-up again.

The combination of babies and deep water frightened me. I was always afraid the horse would hit a snag or stumble while the baby, wriggly at any time, came adrift from his carrier's arms. Ruth shared my fears. Would a tiny baby that couldn't struggle, sink immediately or bob up once or twice to give you the chance to grab it? I think they would go straight to the bottom. Someone suggested to drop one and see but neither of us were that keen to prove our point.

Again we arrived at our destination just before the rain and our lives formed a pattern. Up to Butcher Hill, stop for a muster and go home for awhile. Then we would go up — and back again. As Johnnie grew his folding bassinet was replaced as top-load by a pair of wooden horse-rockers and he made the trip sitting on a cushion in front of Bill's or my saddle — clothed to the top of his head but no umbrella!

Sometimes we were at home long enough to start a garden going and to get the hen-population broken-in to lay in more accessible places. Then we would be gone again and return to a dead garden and an uncivilised poultry flock greatly diminished in number. Rather unaccountably the dingoes and pigs never got the lot.

Mustering was usually done in the rainier time of the year

hence all our horse-back junketings. Dry weather saw us home with Bill working every day to restore the old fences and erect a new set of yards.

When Johnnie was seven months old we bought a windmill and had water laid-on to within a hundred yards of the house. Until Bill packed short lengths of piping from the Normanby battery on his in-disgrace "chase" horses fresh from their defeat at the Laura races, we brought the water closer by coupling the hose to the last length of pipe and sealing the hose with a cork tied across with string like the old yeast bottle. This worked admirably when the tank was half-full but any more water than that and the pressure would "pop" the cork so that an empty tank greeted us.

The house was not left out of the improvements either. A fence was added to segregate humans from poultry and wild pigs, the humans being inside the fence. Another wall was built at the far end and the calico which I had strung on two wires in a square for our "room" and which the wind had down on the floor more times than it was up was replaced, after much procrastination and protest on Bill's part, by three-ply partitions.

Best of all, we acquired Arthur Jones, a retired cattleman and drover, one-time partner with the Roberts in Springvale. With Arthur to stay with me in case of accident or sickness, I was able to remain home when Bill went to Butcher Hill.

We began to milk cows, the two Tableland poddies now with calves of their own. We had no bail and Arthur had one useless hand and a growth on the other which necessitated, later the removal of a finger, but we managed by roping the cows to the rails of an old horse-yard with a loop around the neck and a hind leg. Being quiet, they stood for us. Lacking a calf-pen, the calves were tied up with collars and chains each night so that they couldn't suck their mothers (thus leaving milk for us) and when the dingoes came howling their threats on a moonlit night, Arthur took his swag over and camped beside the calves.

From time to time, our neighbours came over, but as Gladys went out mustering with Jock, there wasn't much time for social calls. They called in to see all was well if they were passing and would ride over with split-bags over the bags of their saddles loaded with fresh beef, vegetables, milk and eggs when we had none and often a freshly-caught barramundi from the long lagoon in front of their house.

Meanwhile, with fences to hold our growing herd, Bill's thoughts turned to droving to earn that extra money to keep us until our herd grew sufficiently to pay our bills. Lakefield was to put off a mob of cattle. If they were to go overland, Bill was to have the droving.

"If you like," offered Bill's mother, "I'll mind baby John and you can go too. It will save a Mission boy's wages."

I thought of leaving the little fellow behind — I thought of more separation from Bill. I weighed the advantages of a soft, dry bed against a hard, wet swag and a leaking tent and I said, "Yes, please."

But it didn't work out that way. The Lakefield cattle went by the new cattle-barge "Wewak" to the meatworks in Cairns. Instead we went mustering to Sand Flat with Miles Morris.

Bill's mother kept her promise — conditionally. I could go only if I had got over my new batch of morning-sickness by January. Miraculously, my twenty-four hour a day misery ended with the old year and I was able to ride off with Bill. There were just the two of us — and our plant horses.

At Maitland, we picked up Miles and his two boys and left there together, gathering up a few coachers as we neared our mustering destination. There is a saying among the local stock-boys. "When you too young, you tail. When you too bloody old, you tail."

To that I'd like to add "When you are the female of the species you always tail." Tailing is a kind of baby-sitting, only you baby-sit cattle. It is the tailer's job to hold the quiet — or relatively so — cattle in a handy position at a creek junction or on a river flat, while the more favoured musterers scout out for more cattle.

These they wheel, galloping, into the coachers and once in, it is the tailer's job to keep them in until the last of the wild ones have been accounted for. Then you move the combined mob on to the next waiting place.

We would ride out early, letting the coachers out of the yard at first light and would start driving them to wherever we were to muster. Each man watched carefully for cattle signs, for fresh tracks or recent cattle-camps. It was a great feeling to ride out early and smell the hot, steamy, not totally unattractive odour left where cattle had camped the night before. At least they couldn't be too far ahead of us.

It being mountainous country, the cattle preferred the rivers and the low ridges bordering them so we invariably followed the streams.

Some days we followed the creeks up — other days we ran them down — but always it fell to the same pattern. The man riding in the lead would motion us to stop, pointing up a creek or over a hill to indicate cattle had passed that way a matter of hours ago. Then Bill would ride back to tell us to wait.

He could have saved his energy for we tailers knew just what to expect when tracks were found at creek junctions.

"Tracks gone up that way. Do you think you and Arthur (a one-eyed black-boy this time) can hold them here? 'Bye." And in parting, "Don't go to sleep and lose any."

Arthur was a past-master at tailing and at doing contortions on horse-back. As soon as Miles and Bill were gone he would select a shady tree and ride up under it. He would take his feet from the stirrup-irons and cross them behind the saddle, legs trailing over his horse's rump. Then he would fold his arms across his horse's wither, drop his chin onto them comfortably and doze off. Somehow he seemed to be able to ignore the ups and downs of a stock-saddle and the general effect looked quite restful.I tried to copy it but never got it right. The pommel and the cantle of my saddle got in the road.

Sometimes the men would be away for hours. In that case, Arthur would dismount to have a sounder sleep and I would begin to eat my dinner, piece by piece, with intervals between courses when I rode to turn-back an obstreperous coacher or two. Soggy damper, soaked through with jam or syrup is not particularly appetising but it does help pass the time and whatever else may be said against it, it is undeniably "filling."

One evening as we were sitting around the fire at a camp right on the highway, a man drove up, very unseasonably, in an old utility truck to ask the way to Maitland. Miles obliged with the directions. (It's manners not to ask questions). Then it appeared the man was a prospective buyer, so it was decided Miles would take a couple of days off to show him around.

In the meantime, we mustered close at hand, the places where it was less likely to find cattle in any numbers.

I met the buyer returning as I was riding in to camp to put on our damper and stew. He stopped his ute and introduced me to his wife and children then settled for a bit of a chat.

Ranger, who distrusted horseless-carriages, was not going to be lured too close. The conversation was carried on at what I thought was a safe distance with Ranger, by the feel of him, ready to leave without a moment's notice. Every so often, one of the small fry would pop a head around the home-made canopy at the back and just as suddenly pop back again. This, Ranger found disconcerting.

In the distance we could hear the sound of cattle being driven so the buyer and I decided we would best be going on our ways.

"Have you any matches?" he asked. "I'm on my last."

There were none in our swag at the camp so I tossed my tin to him.

"Thanks. Well, be seeing you!"

Crash, he slammed his door. Ranger jumped and I nearly followed the trajectory path of my matches onto the buyer's lap. The kids popped out all at once and roared their appreciation but I had left at an undignified pace for the river.

It was heartening to meet the buyer's wife by chance in Mareeba some years later and we spoke of Maitland and the place that they did finally buy.

"Remember that day we met you? The kids were thrilled to bits. You were their first real live cowgirl."

I shifted Nancy to the other hip, changed my string bag to the other hand, disentangled Johnnie from my skirts and smirked.

"And when you made your horse rear up for them before you galloped away, they went wild. We heard nothing but you for weeks."

Thinking over the incident, it was good to think someone thought our act was intentional and gratifying to know someone enjoyed it.

Being a tailer had many disadvantages. It was monotonous — the perfect training ground for patience. It was hard to keep alert hour upon hour upon hour. False alarms there were in plenty. We would think the men were coming, rein our horses up and have them ready for action and no one would appear. Then they would come, unexpectedly, and their cattle would be upon us before we knew what was going on.

One day, while I was holding the cattle on my own for some reason, it drizzled rain all day, the kind that finds every leak in your raincoat and trickles from hat-brim to collar, seeping from there in an advancing cold-front over shivering ribs and shoulder-blades. My horse was continually trying to back rump-on into the direction of the rain and the cattle tried to shelter in shrubby scrubs. It was a beautiful day!

Some cattle were walking through the bushes on the river-bank just below me. Sure that they must have been some of my coachers walking off, I went after them, to stop dead in my tracks — they were all cleanskins! Seven of them.

Then how the minutes dragged! I strained eyes and ears hoping for some sign of the men returning for I couldn't leave the coachers. Nor would I have been able to do anything useful if I could. I was forced to sit in the drizzle and watch the cleanskins as they fed about unconcerned, picking at the couch grass along the river. Then they leisurely had a drink, filed up the other bank and walked away.

My cattle lay in their scrubby shelter and maddeningly

chewed their contented cuds. It wouldn't have hurt them to have bellowed a little and tried to call the others in! I seethed in my inability to do anything and the men returned empty-handed.

It was too late to go after the ones I had seen. There was just time left to get to camp by dark so we rode home silently to be met by a cloud-burst on our way. We had to swim the little creek at the camp and found that the rain had overflowed the gutters we'd dug around the tents and turned the cream of tartar and soda in the pack-bags to a liquid consistency. Swags were soaked. Matches wouldn't strike and the fire could not keep alight long enough to boil the billy.

Miles's horse ran a stake into his hoof and one of Bill's had broken a hobble-strap and cleared out. Truly a grey day. Almost unbelievably we were given a second chance. We met the seven cleanskins later and went home with them in the mob.

While being a tailer, pushing coachers in and out of flooded creeks in order to get them to a strategic position in time doesn't hold many advantages, being the only woman in the camp and a Boss's wife to boot, carries a few.

After being an under-strapper for so long, I gloried in the privileges open to me now in my higher status. The best was that I could leave the cattle a mile or two from camp and ride in, alone and untrammelled. I could even canter all the way if I wished for my horses were my own. It was great to be able to say to Arthur and (black) Norman, "You fellows right? I'll go on in." And then ride away in time to have an unhurried bogey (swim) in the creek before settling to the business of getting tea ready.

Miles didn't sell Maitland so he had to get back home again. So did we so we started back driving a goodly-sized mob before us. At Maitland we cut out, dividing equally between the two camps and Bill and I set off down the range with our share.

It was dark just after we reached the foot of the range but we had about two miles to go to reach the yard where we were to camp. I could tell where Bill was for he was playing cowboy songs in a high-pitched tone on a leaf but keeping track of the cattle and horses was not quite as easy. Now and then a snapped stick or a kicked stone would send one of us after a beast that was walking away or a steady 'chump-chump' would lead to a cow feeding off down the river.

Needless to say, although the muster had been a good one and a pleasant change to a housewife's life it was good to be back at the station. Johnnie had his first birthday the day before we arrived back and was able to walk a few drunken-sailor steps to meet us. I;'d had a break and was ready for domesticity again.

But the Boss had other ideas.

He wanted to muster around the homestead and an extra man would be handy. Bill's old saddle-horse Pigeon was in the paddock, shod-up all-round and lacking only a rider. Thinking it would only mean a few rides out from the house I buckled my bridle around Pigeon's throat.

I was, of course, mistaken. The Boss, after mustering the paddocks was heading for the Normanby. He was still short-handed. Pigeon was very fat, fresh and shod all-round and I, apart from looking after one baby and producing another, was doing nothing useful at all.

Not having an answer to this argument I kissed Johnnie goodbye and rode off after the others.

# 16.

# NOTHING LIKE A GOOD BRISK WALK

Ruth had not long returned from her year's work as stud-groom at Fenwick and was finding the bush rather a hard place after the lights of Melbourne. She was also encountering romantic storms and was becoming engaged, either officially or unofficially, to quite a number of Prince Charmings.

She had also come back from Fenwick with an Arab stallion and had dreams of a "place of her own" in which the stallion figured prominently. At the time, apart from worrying what she was going to do with the stallion, she was in dire straights trying to handle concurrently three admirers with serious intentions. All this tended to make her a little absent-minded when the Normanby muster was being discussed.

Bill's other sister Joy who lived at Laura Station was also expecting a second child and Ruth was taking her aunthood very seriously. She was collecting any article concerning babies and motherhood that came her way.

In one of the newspapers we used for dinner wrapping paper she had found a list of names and their meanings printed to help prospective parents make a selection. Ruth entered into the name-choosing game with great gusto. She carried the pages neatly folded to fit in her shirt pocket and would check with Edwin before coming to me with the short list.

The names chosen were all for a girl and had a distinct Spanish flavour. Bonita headed the list but Juanita, Chiquita, Rosita and even Carmencita were on it.

Seeing I wasn't terribly receptive to the suggestions, Ruth rode off in a huff putting her names back in her pocket and telling me she'd use them for her Arab fillies.

Ruth loved giving advice and it wasn't long before she was back. This time with a slightly larger folder on "Advice to the Expectant Mother". It was too big for the shirt pocket but it fitted easily in her saddle-bag from which it could be removed for consultation when Ruth thought fit.

While my favourite bit of advice was the one suggesting husbands take their wives early morning cups of tea in bed, Ruth, years away from motherhood fancied excerpts more in the line of "healthy exercise", "long, brisk walks" and "cold not HOT baths". Anything to make an uncomfortable lot a whole lot more uncomfortable.

The only thing that saved me from a "long brisk walk" each evening after we got back to camp was that my tormentor was as tired as I was. By the time we had walked half-a-mile downhill over loose rocks to bathe and walked back what seemed like a mile carrying a billycan of water in each free hand, the urge to walk briskly, even for a short distance was gone. Unfortunately there were no hot springs about so cold baths were the only ones offering.

What finally cured Ruth of her walk-and-freeze tactics was a day spent disastrously in doing much and getting nowhere.

We were to muster behind the scrubs, a point just upstream from where we had lost the cow and calf from the coachers. For more than half a day we followed tracks, never getting closer to anything but more tracks.

Finally, the elusive "tracks" separated. Bill and Paddy took one lot and the Boss, Ruth and I took the others. Ours turned out to be three quiet bullocks. Theirs, presumably, were "wild" cattle for they never sighted them.

We saw our cattle on a high stony ridge, going the wrong way

— the way that led to the "wild" Normanby.

"Block them," said the Boss.

Ruth and I raced to get to the lead of them. The Boss cantered away steadily along the bottom of the hill in the direction the bullocks should take. The cattle, by nature of their leading position had first choice and they chose the narrow pad negotiating the hillside. We were forced to try to get around them by galloping up the steep, rocky sides of the ridge.

Our horses had been fat and fresh at the start of the day which was a hot, steamy one. They were fresh no longer from going up hill and down again all morning and, as for being fat — they were too fat. They knocked-up.

The bullocks, seeing we were falling back rather than gaining on them, obligingly ended their little game and dropped first to a trot and then to a slow jog. We had so nearly got to the lead of them that it was frustrating not to be able to go that little bit extra and get them.

Our horses were blundering and stumbling. They were black with sweat. It dripped from them to the ground, mixing with the blood our spurs had drawn. Their sides heaved and their nostrils were fully expanded. They were "done".

From below came the encouraging cry, "Block 'em. Block 'em. BLOCK 'EM!"

There was nothing to do but to dismount. We did. With loosened girths the horses stood while the cattle paused in surprise to see us on foot and by doing so gave the Boss time to slip around from his side of the hill and 'block them'. He held them up for a few minutes and then they turned and trotted down the "right" side of the watershed to where the quiet cattle ran.

Once more we were in disgrace. The Boss did not even come round to see where we were but just rode off, mission accomplished, his horse stepping lightly and shying gaily at a rock wallaby we had disturbed as we went down the slope.

With a nervous giggle, Ruth turned to me and said, "Now for a long brisk walk."

We began our descent but you could hardly call it "walking". We slid, climbed down backwards, stumbled, rolled when a horse staggered on to us and upset our precarious equilibrium and we crawled. Our horses, at times stretched out on a tight rein behind us, often raced past creating an avalanche to have us on a tight rein behind them. Our spurs became tangled in vines and tripped us. A wild boar, frightened by our noisy progress as he rooted in the rocks, rushed blindly in Ruth's direction, frightening us in his turn.

Rocks bounced off rocks within inches of our persons as the weary horses caused baby land-slides as they slipped and slid along the loose stones and vines. With all the rocks handy it was a good chance to do a bit of prospecting but we never thought of it at the time.

By the time we reached the bottom we were a tearful pair. The Boss would certainly have something to say about having to block the bullocks after which he had sent us.

We felt rejected and unloved. Which of course was a downright untruth. Ruth's problem was in being loved by too many at once and I had no reason to think Bill's affection had withered.

Still, it was a comfort to be able to feel good and miserable where no one could see us (and laugh) so we sniffed and snuffled to our broken-hearts' content until we cheered up.

Then Ruth saw the blood on her mare's shoulder where she had been spurring her in a vain effort to get her going and was overcome with tearful remorse. With a liberal measure of tears and spit applied with her shirt-tail she cleared away the traces of her cruelty. I was also amazed to see blood on Pigeon's ribs for though I wore spurs, I rarely used them.

We had removed our spurs on the cliff-front and now we were on reasonably level ground so we put them on once more and re-mounted. The Boss was well out of sight by this and wasn't waiting. We could track him easily by sound as his mare disturbed a rock in the creek-bed or danced around on loose stones to evade the usual "livening-up" for stumbling.

Half-way to the creek junction the Boss was joined by Bill and Paddy looking almost as dejected as we felt. They had found nothing. While they reported this we were able to catch-up a little but Bill, I noticed with the suspicion of another sniff coming, did not even turn his head to look back at me, let alone ride back to join me.

Pigeon and I kept plugging along in mutual misery, neither of us improving with time. I wondered, fleetingly, why the advisory lady had cited horse-riding ("in the early months") as healthy exercise.

Twice Pigeon fell badly on rocks cutting her stifle and pulling off a hind shoe but I was so far behind no one saw. Or cared.

Ruth, who was further advanced than I in the Indian file, was sent with Paddy to get supper. I suppose if I had been closer I could have gone too — Pigeon willing. Instead, I trailed further behind.

As we got to the river near the camp, the men splashed out of the water just as Pigeon and I entered it. She hit a rock the first step she took and blundered right down. I was about to jump clear when she lunged above the surface once more. Both of us were wet.

"Oh, well," I tried to console myself, "cold baths are best."

I got within sight of the camp just as Bill had let his horse go and was preparing to go down the river for a swim. I would have to be quick to catch him so I called, "Mate, would you put another shoe on Pigeon for me, please?"

While he got his shoeing gear I was able to get her to the saddle-rack and remove her saddle ready for him to begin. I held her while Bill tried to tack on the shoe. Feeling a bit ashamed of our tearful session (which had not been missed by the Boss after all for he told us with a wicked gleam in his eye that the river rose six inches while we rode home) I just told Bill, Pigeon knocked-up and fell and twisted a shoe off. I may as well have saved my breath as he wasn't listening.

As I held Pigeon and Bill had her hind leg off the ground, she leant on me, her neck over my shoulder so that I took a considerable part of her weight. Judging by the way Bill was muttering through his mouthful of nails, I gathered he was supporting a good half of Pigeon as well.

He persevered a little longer, then suddenly dropped Pigeon's hoof and stepped aside. Unsupported at that end, Pigeon crumpled to the ground.

"Ha," I thought. "That'll learn him!" But I was soon checked.

"This mare's knocked-up! Why didn't you tell me she was knocked-up!"

"I tried to," I wailed, feeling bad again but Bill's thoughts and his sympathy were with Pigeon, his ex-saddle mare.

I took her bridle off and let her go where she stood and was reprimanded for that, too. She stood there all night, head down with never a bite of grass, a sip of water or a wink of sleep. Her ex-boss took her to water in the morning and left her on the couch grass there.

Ruth had her troubles, too. For the second time running her freshly-baked damper had disappeared overnight. The first time the 'possums got the blame as there were dozens of them hidden out in hollow limbs around the camp. The second night Ruth heard her dog being sick and went to see what was wrong.

Her sympathy soon converted to annoyance and we were awoken to thumps, bangs and loud yelps before she dragged the culprit off and put him on a more secure chain for the night.

"It was bad enough just stealing my dampers," she complained. "Why did he have to sick one up!" The final insult rankled.

Meanwhile, sixty crooked miles away at Laura Station, Joyce was getting her early morning tea in bed. Her second baby was due six weeks after ours but the best-laid plans go haywire at times and Mary made an entrance in Atherton two days before Nancy. Weighing-in at nine and a half pounds, Nancy opened her blue eyes on the beauties of Cooktown.

"Cowgirls" at a Laura sports meeting – Shirley Porter, Ruth Shephard, and Connie Gostelow.

Father and son – Bill and Johnnie.

Maurice Shephard and Myles Gostelow, officials at Laura sports, 1960.

Packing the plant at Old Fairview yards.

Ruth Shephard and helper Leo, loaded up.

Palmerville camp at Laura Races.

"There," soothed Ruth, sympathising with my long wait and appreciative of Nancy's birth-weight, "what did I say about brisk walks being good for you?"

# 17.

# WE LEASE A MOUNTAIN STATION AND GO DROVING

We did not return home immediately after the Normanby muster. Bill and I went up with another neighbour to muster his "wild" country camping at one camp with the romantic name of "Moonrise".

That done, Johnnie and I went home to stay while Bill remained to help in yet another muster at Butcher Hill.

The night that they finished with the cattle after that muster, he rode home getting to Harvest Home just after midnight. I was used to his nocturnal comings and goings — they were necessary if I were to see him at all — but I wasn't prepared for the news he had.

Unlike me, Bill can keep news to himself indefinitely. He said nothing while I re-lit the fire and prepared a belated supper. He waited until we had retired then, just as I was on the brink of sleep, he delivered his piece of information.

"Well, mate, we have a station."

"What?" I cried, very quickly leaping back from the shades of slumber. "Where?"

We had been trying rather hopelessly for a suitable block of unimproved Crown land and had lightly considered partnerships in existing properties. Harvest Home was getting a bit too small for our growing herd.

"Dad said we could have the country below the Block!"

The Boss wasn't there so the best I could do was to kiss his proxy. Bill was certainly the bearer of glad tidings. For the remaining hours of darkness we talked of our good fortune with Bill for once keeping up his share of the conversation.

We were to sub-lease the country on the Laura side of the fence, paying for the rates and rents and for any improvements we wanted to make. As well as the country we could have some of the cattle. These were mainly milkers' 'calves' that weren't wanted in the milking mob or cattle from the Normanby, put there to stop them going back.

The Boss was keeping the bulls and the spayed cows. There were few bullocks as when weaned most steers were turned out on the black soil. As soon as an agreement was drawn up we could start branding the calves with our brand and could take cattle down from our heavily stocked paddocks at Harvest Home.

It wasn't top country. There were no improvements save a small dam, a broken-down brumby yard and another yard in good order but our luck had changed. Our beloved Block of all places! I told myself, "This year it will be different. I'll see more of Bill. No need for him to go away so much."

So much for wishful thinking. Nothing could have been further from the truth.

Life went on its same uneventful course after Nancy was born. We still trekked back and forth from home to Butcher Hill but this time, Nancy being a dry-weather baby, we usually travelled in style in the old truck. Unfortunately, at this time, due to some change in the chemical content of petrol, most trucks were developing "fuel trouble" or vaporisation. Our truck was no exception so that while we may have left home by truck, we usually arrived at our destination on foot, with two babes-in-arms and a sugar-bag full of baby clothes that couldn't be left behind.

However, with Arthur to "go for help" if needed, I could quite safely stay home and after I had done my duty and shown the baby to her grandparents, this is what I did.

While I was away, Bill had effected a few improvements at home. I was very pleasantly surprised to come back to concrete on part of the floor, a lean-to wash-house complete with my concrete tubs proudly in place on a bush-timber stand and, best of all, water laid on with three taps for the house.

I saw very little of Ruth who had sorted-out her heart-throbs, rejected the lot and found a new one.

"He's like Bill," she decided, "nice and old-fashioned."

His rather conservative nature had earned him, at twenty-three, the nick-name of "Old Saltbush". His name was Fred Shephard and his people too had come to the Peninsula in the days of the Palmer gold-rush.

He had Ruth unnaturally meek and mild, carrying out his every wish without argument.

No shorts to be worn! Right. Ruth bundled up the offending garments and sent them to Iris who was under no such ban. No dresses without adequately covered tops was the next decree. Leo got the ones that failed to pass muster.

Never had Ruth obeyed orders so swiftly and so submissively. Everyone breathed a sigh of relief and said, "It must be love this time." Ruth added the final words on the subject, "It must be the real thing. Freddie isn't very handsome and you ought to hear him try to sing cowboy songs!"

They were married when Nancy was nine months old.

A few months before that, not long after the Boss had given us the country below the Block, Hardy and Iris went up to Merluna, a big run north-west of Coen, isolated for most of the year from anywhere else, but very good cattle country.

Iris' baby girl was born there. They had moved in without any trouble but the storms and then the Wet came and they could not get out. Making the best of a bad situation, they arranged for a trained ex-nurse living on a mining field adjacent to, but miles from, Merluna to help out. She came over, officiated at the birth and an ensuing haemorrhage but had to return to her own family before Iris was really well. Iris' next baby was born in civilisation.

Hardy was having a hard time mustering the cattle which had to be sold. He had over two thousand square miles of country and very little knowledge of it — where the yards were, where cattle could water and so on. Most of the horses were pensioners and there weren't enough to ride and the native stockmen who had more or less had the place to themselves in recent years didn't want to co-operate with a new "Boss".

Bill flew up to Coen to give Hardy a hand with the first muster to get a mob ready for the road. Freddie, with Ruth, his sister Thelma and some of their station "boys" were to take the mob to the sale-yards at Mareeba.

The girls came half-way with the cattle, as far as Laura, when Thelma's mother became ill and she had to return home. Ruth, now unchaperoned, returned with her. She was bitterly disappointed but also was worried how Fred would get on with two drovers short.

Another mob was to leave Merluna about the time of Ruth and Fred's wedding. Since Hardy was mustering, he was unable to attend the wedding but arrangements were made for the newly-wed pair to leave Cooktown the day after the ceremony and fly to Coen to take delivery of the Merluna cattle there.

While others were sadly sympathetic, the bride was delighted. Here was her heart's desire — Freddie and the opportunity to "go droving". Fred was not quite as enthusiastic and was relieved when a telegram came from Hardy as a reprieve — "cattle delayed".

When they did come down there were two mobs. One Fred had contract-mustered and a second one, both of them with over a thousand head. Bill was to take the first mob, giving Fred time to go home and get a fresh plant of horses before he returned to take the second one.

Bill's cattle were to move in January after the storms had fallen and the stock route was in good order again with reasonable grass and water available.

He was away when the telegram arrived in the mail. It had been sent three weeks before from Coen. Hardy wanted Bill to meet the cattle in Coen in early December so the cattle would reach Mareeba for the first sale of the year. It was now mid-November!

The drovers Bill had tentatively signed-on for January couldn't get away any earlier. The Mission was reluctant to let boys leave for outside work over the Christmas period. No one else seemed to be much interested in working over Christmas either but two young tin-miners, cousins whose hobby was horses, said they'd come. Finally the Mission sent three boys, one with experience and two without and Bill picked up 'old' John, as drover's cook, from Laura.

Seven hands for an expected mob of twelve hundred mixed cattle — bulls, piker bullocks, stags, cows, heifers, steers and new-born calves! It was not enough to bring down a mob over a rough route which experienced drovers considered was capable of handling mobs of up to eight hundred.

There seemed to be no alternative but for me to roll my swag again. A friend agreed to look after Nancy. Her own daughter was the same age. Arthur would probably be happier without me at Harvest Home and John left in high glee bound for Butcher Hill with his grandfather. I took the railmotor from Cooktown to Laura after leaving Nancy with Dawn. The three Mission boys were on the same motor so Bill was able to pick us all up together.

It should have taken us less than three weeks to come back from Coen to Laura with the cattle but three weeks' supplies for eight, plus swags, tents, pack-covers, cooking gear, etc., made a heavy load so Fred's brother, who was returning to Musgrave with adequate room on his truck, kindly took most of our loading up with him. He also took his uncle — our cook.

We took only enough to get to Musgrave, re-stocked there and took what we thought was enough tucker to get us up to Hardy and back to Musgrave. It was a great saving in horse-power especially as no rain had fallen and grass and water were in short supply.

The heat was terrific as we left Laura and to make things

worse I didn't feel well. Headaches, aching joints and light-headedness. I put it down to the heat. At times I'd feel reasonably well but then the aches would start again. At Fairview, the telegraph repeater station, they recorded fourteen consecutive days with a temperature of over 100° Fahrenheit, then a break of a day and off for another ten days of over century heat until the mercury again dropped — temporarily. It seemed even hotter than that!

In order to meet Hardy on time we were forced to do long stages, but our horses had only dry-weather condition behind them and with no grass and very little water along the route they soon weakened. Our first casualty occurred the second day out from Laura. Faithful little Growler, willing worker, loyal friend, became over-heated and died on a twenty-three mile stretch without water. We carried her for quite some way hoping to find water in time to save her but we did not. On our return all that remained of her was a pitiful handful of ginger hair and a few small bones by the roadside.

Getting the plant ready at short notice, we had managed to muster only enough horses to do the trip, allowing two horses each, four night-horses, eight packs and six spares. We soon found they were not enough.

When pack-horses — and even one mule! — knocked-up, Bill packed saddle-horses and when saddle-horses ran short, Bill pulled up for a day on a running spring, killed for fresh meat and broke-in a fat pack-mare to ride using a small station-owned yard on the ridge to work in.

Even then, we had occasionally to ride pack-horses and had to buy re-inforcements generously offered by others who were not too well supplied themselves. With them, we got through until the rain came and, despite all this and three horses being poisoned — none fatally (one by a plant and two with over-strength dip) we arrived home with all of them.

Hardy was camped one night out from Coen, on a creek running into the Gulf, when we met him. He counted the cattle out to Bill after we started them off dinner-camp and strung them down the Port Stewart Range.

"Eleven hundred and five," he counted looking at the last beast, a hundred yards behind the rest, poor, lame, ears drooped and saliva hanging in strings from its mouth. "They're all yours and I think that one" indicating the straggler, "has Three Day Sickness."

It had — and so did the other eleven hundred and four, once, twice and sometimes three times each before they reached Mareeba. Three Day Sickness is another name for Ephemeral Fever and if that means nothing to you, well, at that stage it didn't mean anything to us either.

The disease had hit the Peninsula very lightly thirty years before but no fatalities were recorded and no one thought much of the outbreak. Now it had broken out all over the northern part of the State and the Government vets kept giving advice to rest the afflicted animals on abundant grass with water in easy reach. On no account were the affected animals to be driven.

Unfortunately ours had no grass, no water and we had to move them. On leaving each night-camp and each dinner-camp usually at least one beast had to be helped to its feet and steadied until its legs could support it. The heat didn't help and the poorer, weaker cattle on the tail were so frightened to lie down in case they couldn't get up, that one old bony stag died on his feet. He collapsed after death, just falling sideways to the ground.

The few fat cattle in the mob were affected worse than the boners but Three Day Sickness wasn't our only worry. The cattle had blight — some were blind in both eyes and stumbled in and out of the mob and in and out of break-away gullies with routine repetition. Many more were lame with foot-rot, their legs above the hoof swollen and red, the skin stretched almost to bursting point. Each step brought excruciating agony until the swelling burst, the hoof "fell off", or the animal died.

To add to the burden of straws already laid across the camel's back, a big percentage of the cows were calving. As it was absolutely impossible to take the calves along, they had to be killed as soon after birth as possible — a duty the men abhorred but there was no alternative.

A few lucky calves survived to be carried in to homesteads and given to the children to rear with the milkers. This was often the first start to their own herd of cattle. The distraught mothers tried every night to go back to where they had last suckled their babies. Most of the time they succeeded in getting away in the darkness and had to be found and driven back to the mob again the following day.

A few went back twenty miles to their dead calves — too far for our weakened horses to retrieve them.

We tried the old dodge of carrying the pelts of the dead calves but these cows refused to be fooled. They wanted calves — not calf-skins.

Then there were the cattle injured when they had rushed a yard before we took delivery — a calf with part of its gut protruding through a hole near its ribs (we left it on the first combination of grass and water that we found and it survived) — cows which calved grotesquely huge dead calves, swollen and fetid — and pikers and cows alike with horn wounds suppurating under elbows and on shoulders.

And there were bulls, dozens of them. Big, brave fellows they were on their home run, full of strength and fight, but off their own territory they began, one by one, to give up the fight and for no apparent reason often lay down and refused to move. On the other hand, the rest battled on under what should have been unsurmountable difficulties and, when the rain came and made fresh feed, they even brightened up and began to fatten.

Nearly every morning as Bill counted them off camp, the numbers were down. It was disheartening. All hands were doing all they could to get the cattle along that route, slowly and with the lead of the stronger cattle held in check so that the weaker ones could follow along feeding on what little grass there was. No cattle were "lost" but each day saw another one — or more — left behind to take its chance of death or survival.

Drovers are required by law to travel no less than eight miles daily in order to prevent the routes being eaten-out by travelling stock which dwelt too long in the "long paddock".

Some days we managed six miles. Some days we covered two and, when we did find water enough for the whole mob, we sometimes spelled a day or an afternoon to give them a chance to rest.

The heat was killing. Cattle were put on dinner-camp at 11 a.m. but at 4 p.m. they were still "tonguing", the bovine equivalent to sweating, with the heat. The unfortunate animals on the tail were pitiful. To move was all they could manage. There was neither time nor energy to eat the few stalks of stubbly grass and when they did find water, often at two-day intervals, it had usually been stirred to mud by the first thousand head and they would turn away without drinking.

The sick and the lame gravitated to the tail so that they almost became a separate mob. With Bill spending most of his time going back for calf-less mother-cows, the care of the cripples fell to me. I suffered with them. They moved so slowly, every step having to be forced from them, that I often led my horse to spell him and drove them on foot, sometimes pulling back on an old bull's tail to make him take a few steps ahead to avoid the contact.

The natives in the Peninsula use the powdered roots of the fresh-water mangrove to drug fish in a water-hole. After it is powdered it is scattered on the surface of the water and the stupefied fish float to the top where they are easily collected. Drovers unintentionally use the same principal but for them mud does the work of the drug.

Driving a large mob of cattle through a shallow water-hole soon churns up the muddy bottom and, again, the fish surface. We dined on roasted "long-toms", a type of pike, succulent perch and delicious coal-baked yabbies to augment the dullness of damper, "oil" and jam. The cook, coming behind us to get water to take on to the next dry camp, took also a sugar-bag of fish, the bigger ones which succumbed later, for our supper.

Usually when water was scarce the pack-horse men carried it in five gallon canteens slung one each side of the water-can horse.

From these they left us an inadequate billyful for our dinner camp. At times they had to go back several miles from where we had camped to get water to take on, past that camp, to the next one. At times like that, they could spare none for us. One day, six of us and Bulldog, Growler's son, had five not-quite-full beer bottles of bully-frog infested water to last us all day. When we did come to water that evening — in shallow wheel-tracks on the road — I would willingly have drunk the tadpoles too, if necessary.

Bill used his horn-saw to cut into the bulges on tea-trees. Water trickled out enticingly from the cut, icy, wet, clear — and salty! We tried several trees but never found any with drinkable water. We drank lots of undrinkable water, green and scummy, full of pig-tracks and at times with dead beasts bogged not far enough away. Surprisingly we suffered no ill-effects.

Washing was a problem. The men, for the most part, stuffed their dirty clothes into the pockets of their swags, selecting from these when all clean ones were exhausted, the ones that smelt the least. I carried a sugar-bag of our dirty clothes and a bar of soap until the soap crumbled and the pommel of my saddle nearly rubbed through the bag before I found enough water to wash, or half-wash, our clothes.

Each day brought us just that little bit closer to the saleyards and to rain. Storms often fell behind us, the lightning from them illuminating where we were, but no rain fell. An odd storm fell ahead of us but, long before we reached it, the sun had dried up both water and grass.

Each day as the weaker animals dropped out we were left with a slightly stronger mob but for each one gone, another dropped back to the tail to take its place.

The nights were mostly overcast making it impossible to see the cattle in the dark. The night-watch used torches to bring recalcitrant beasts back into the mob and with the cattle discontented and restless — especially if they could smell a pint of sludge from a near-by bog-hole — we had to double-watch, two men going on at a time.

I usually took first watch riding my own saddle horse around and around, pushing in the strays that fed out and trying to get them all down and sleeping by the time the real first watch came out on night-horses to relieve me. The more cattle that were down camping, the more pleased they were. Sometimes I rode for twenty minutes. Sometimes I fell in and out of burnt-out messmate stump-holes for two hours trying to dodge the slightly-more-visible fallen timber.

We watched from about 7 p.m. when the cattle were first put on camp until 4 a.m. when the camp was called and the horse-tailer went for the horses while we had breakfast.

Bill and Archie, the one Mission boy with experience, took the middle watch, for it is then that the cattle may get up and walk around a bit before settling down for the rest of the night. Archie had been Uncle Bill's main man during his later droving years and could tell many a comic tale of their doings on the road.

Bill played his gum-leaf to the cattle. The Mission boys harmonised hill-billy songs that were really worth listening to — if only you could stay awake to listen.

Occasionally an odd beast would come into camp looking for water, step carefully among the sleepers in their rolled-out swags and walk out again before the night-watch came around. As well as having to be careful that no droving cattle strayed out, the watch had to be equally careful that no "bush" cattle came in. The watch kept awake by frequent calls on the big billy of coffee stewing beside the fire but even then it was all too easy to drop off to sleep as the night-horse paced steadily, around and around and around.

Always the camp was placed on the Coen side of the cattle so that any would-be run-aways would have to pass the fire, the tents and the spare night-horses, patiently waiting their turn, to make their escape.

The cattle soon became used to the camp. With ten days on the road from Merluna to Coen, they were broken-in before we took them over. In the evenings, you could notice a change in them as they heard the bells on the plant-horses feeding about the camp — a sort of metaphorical pricking-of-the-ears — and once the tents came in sight, they would automatically feed over towards them and on to the night-camp.

Once put on camp for the night, the same few would make for the campfire and by the end of the trip they very nearly had to be removed from the coffee billy before the watch could drink.

# 18.

# CHRISTMAS ON THE ROAD

Christmas Day was spent one day north of Musgrave Station and, as we had taken much longer than the calculated time plus an extra allowance, Christmas dinner menu read;

Salt beef.

Damper with fine scrape of syrup.

Weak tea.

After dinner, Bill sent me back to try to get up a sick bullock we had left that morning at a chain of water-holes where we had given the cattle a drink. It was a pleasant spot to spend an afternoon. There was water (possibly a crocodile or two also) and shade, but no matter how hard I tried, I could not get the bullock to stand. His legs seemed to be paralysed and though I could stand him up well enough, neither his legs nor mine could hold him there. Together we'd crumple to the ground.

As I had until dark to get him back to camp I bided my time and waited to try again and again to get him to his feet. The time was filled in between by drinking tea and investigating the cause of the faint "plop plop" noises that seemed to haunt the place.

The noise was made by thousands of well-fed cattle-ticks dropping to the ground. They had fallen from the cattle while they had camped as we had watered them there. The ever-busy meat-ants lost no time in gathering them up and dragging them to the magnetic ant-beds they had usurped.

The ants' working ability and determination far outdid their intelligence. An ant would drag a tick, an enormous burden many times its own weight, for several yards, climb with it up a 70° slope to a hole in the ant-bed and expect the fully engorged tick to fit through a hole big enough to admit ants only!

While the puzzled ant hovered about the doorway, scratching his head and wondering what to do next, a second ant would come hurtling out and the two ants, plus the tick, would drop to the ground, feet below the entrance hole. As this was being repeated dozens of times at different entrances in dozens of ant-beds, the heavy ticks kept up an incessant "Plop, plop, plop" as they fell.

Violetvale Station which owned the lagoons by which the bullock and I waited was the home of the quaint little golden-shouldered ant-bed parrot. These rare parrots, about the size of a peewit, are found, in the Peninsula at least, only in a narrow strip from Port Stewart to just below Musgrave . They live in miniature caverns inside the magnetic ant-beds, reached by tunnels labouriously made by the small birds.

I was delighted as I sat there waiting when a young greenish bird and a brightly painted mature male in his coat of electric blue with touches of black on his head, the golden trademark on his shoulders and a spot of orangey red for underpants, fed some distance away unaware of my presence.

Rosellas and the wildly vivid Blue Mountain parrots were there in numbers. The latter were screeching out their rights to ownership of the Leichhardt apples in the trees shading the lagoons. With the setting of the sun, the little black and white striped honey possums would have something to say for their share but in the daylight the parrots met opposition only from their own ranks.

I waited until almost sundown and made one last attempt to get the bullock to his feet. For a few tottering steps it seemed as if we had succeeded by co-operative effort, then, over-confident he swung his horns around to charge me and toppled to the ground with a grunt.

Leaving him, I rode on to camp getting there in the dark just as Bill was coming back to give me a hand convinced my lateness was due to the fact that I had got the bullock "up" but was having trouble driving him on my own.

The bullock recovered and Fred picked him up when he came down with the second mob, so he went to Mareeba after all.

Reaching camp, I found Hardy was there. He returned with John who had ridden in to give Musgrave notice of our passing. Not unexpectedly, John had been partaking of the Christmas cheer at the station and hadn't quite made it into his swag. Instead he was lying as he fell with the rolled swag under the small of his back, his face up to the cloud-covered moon. Archie and I rearranged him so that he looked a bit more comfortable but he didn't stir until it was time for him to get breakfast.

Besides John, Hardy also brought back a very generous supply of roast beef and plum pudding so we knew for sure, then, that it was Christmas. Christmas or not, the cattle still had to be watched but with Hardy sharing the chore, the watches were shortened a little.

At Musgrave, Ruth was downcast. Fred, returning to Musgrave after mustering the mob we now had, was to go back soon after Christmas to bring the second thousand head down to Mareeba. "Saltbush" Junior was scheduled to make his appearance in a few weeks' time and Ruth had to stay home while Fred did the droving.

I can't say that I didn't envy her lot — or part of it. I t was so beautifully cool under the long-legged house at Musgrave and I was melting away so continuously that I was having trouble keeping my riding trousers from slipping over my hip bones.

Since we were to be paid 30/- for each beast we delivered to the saleyards John used to pretend concern over my boney state by exclaiming at regular intervals, "Can't have you knocking-up halfway."

He'd ladle an extra spoonful of hot curry onto my tin plate

Sisters Ramsay and Paskins who opened the Australian Inland Mission hostel and hospital at Coen in 1958.

Outback children at the A.I.M. Hostel in Coen.

Popular Doris Bassani when she ran the general store in Laura.

despite my protests, with a knowing shake of head and a "Thirty bob is thirty bob you know. Cripes, we can't lose any more!"

To save the thirty shilling loss he seemed to expect, John asked his sister Mary for some of her home-made fever mixture. It was made, said John, of Epsom Salts, quinine, gin, boiled goanna fat and lizards' gizzards. Going by the taste I'd say the first three were present but I wasn't in a sufficiently authorative position to comment on the latter two! Whatever it contained, it did the trick. I was cured and even began to fatten on John's red-hot curries.

In the meantime, I had been receiving worrying reports about Nancy by mulga wire but could not find out for sure what was wrong. I tried to ring from Musgrave but the line to Cooktown was out and we had to move on. The trouble varied from a new tooth to dengue fever and I didn't know whether to try to get down to her or to stay with the cattle. The fact that we were short-handed and that there were no messages at Musgrave from Nancy's temporary foster-mother, tipped the balance to "stay."

After we passed Musgrave we came into country with a little bit of grass but still no water. One night after John left us, the horse-tailer and cook became slewed in the dark while trying to find a native well and spent the night trying to keep together the plant horses they were taking to water. We spent the night without a skerrick of water for tea or coffee, rice or damper, and as they had all the loose horses with them, we spent it with only the horses we had ridden all day for night-horses. And they hadn't had a drink since morning, either.

Tragedy struck us just before this minor mishap. We lost our cook. John had purloined a Musgrave horse — one he had himself run out of a brumby mob years before — to supplement his own meagre horse supply. Once Bill found out about the "loan" he told John to let it go again but instead John decided to take it along "just one more day" until he reached Musgrave's southern boundary.

It was John's invariable and invaluable habit to give Bill a hand each morning to count the cattle off camp as they were gradually started-up and strung-off between the two men. This night, at the wide, sandy Morehead, we had used a Musgrave yard and John was running a trifle late in leaving camp.

Bill was untying the strapped-up rails and I was waiting with him when we heard a scuffle. Looking back, I saw John's horse, the Musgrave brumby, emerge from a cloud of dust with John's saddle. Thinking he had merely pulled away from John I began to chuckle, for John always found much to laugh at in my many predicaments.

I soon stopped as the dust cleared to reveal John on the ground at the base of a huge ironwood tree, I raced over. Bill left the cattle to the boys but Doug was already there. John's head had missed the two feet thick ironwood merely by Providence and perhaps two inches. His face was contorted and a frighteningly purply-blue; he was crying and telling us to take him home.

It was clear that he was not conscious as he began to talk wildly about an assortment of highly irrelevant things as we tried to find out where he was hurt. Appearance couldn't tell us much as John has, in his brief day, broken his neck and been given up for dead, broken arms, a shoulder and legs. He had also lost one kidney and a few feet of intestine to the surgeon's knife, so that his body was as full of lumps, bumps, hills, valleys and ridges as a boarding-house mattress. One side of his body didn't normally correspond with the other.

Also his heart was "a bit crook."

The men carried John carefully and laid him as comfortably as could be managed on his swag in the tucker-tent. Then they left to put the cattle on grass and I remained with John who, thankfully, was speaking normally — joking, laughing, cursing as a "twinge" stabbed at him and demanding tea and A.P.C. powders.

"Can't kill old John," he said rather proudly with a cock-eyed wink but I was far from reassured.

Where he hit ground, there was a deep triangular dent made by his shoulder and with it aching, his arm swelling, his head throbbing, his lips going blue and his face imitating a chameleon or a rainbow, it didn't pay to tempt Providence.

Things weren't too good but they could have been worse. The night before the accident we had entertained a visitor and he — and his tractor — were still there. Hank had driven over on his trusty Fergie from his bachelor home to see his old crony, John, to have a yarn with people in general and to give us some "important mail" to hand in to be posted at Kalinga, the next homestead.

At home, there was a trailer for the tractor so Hank set off as soon as he was reassured his old mate was still living, to get the trailer, a mattress and enough petrol to get them to an emergency airstrip — a claypan — at Kalinga.

While Hank was away, the Gostelows of Kalinga came past, heading home from a visit to Musgrave. It was too far to carry John from the drovers' camp to the road so we waited for Hank and the trusty tractor. Bowie Gostelow, too, was an old mate of John's and John brightened up a bit more so that with Bowie there too, I began to feel a little easier.

One of the Gostelow boys had his arm in a brand-new sling. He had fallen from a mango tree at Musgrave but his dad had splinted it there and then, bush-fashion, and it was giving him no trouble.

"Hmm," remarked our patient. "Two accidents! Who's next?"

I was wondering the same thing myself but it wasn't to be one of us. The ambulance 'plane flew to Musgrave for Matt Gostelow of Violetvale who had done considerable damage to his fore-arm when a quarter of beef he was hanging-up slipped, the steel beef-hook ploughing a furrow in his arm.

John, between despondent spells when he thought of us being left even "shorter-handed", was elated at the thought of seeing Bowie again and was joking about how he planned it all to get away from those so-and-so apologies for cattle, as we lifted him onto the back of the trailer.

Again he turned blue and lost consciousness; not for long, but for long enough to give us a bad fright at least! Nor was it at all re-assuring when he made a repeat performance of it when they transferred him to the truck. We had our doubts whether we'd see our poor old mate again.

But we did. The truck passed us again when we had the cattle back on the motor road and John looked very comfortable lying back on his swag, entertaining the children, two new-born calves snuggling either side of his legs as pillows to hold him steady before they commenced their careers as children's poddies. He looked so cheerful we thought our fears were groundless — stronger than that, we knew they were.

The aerial ambulance took him to hospital in Cairns where they found he had again damaged his shoulder and upper arm. No mention of his heart condition was made but he was in good hands.

As we passed the little "strip" from which the small plane had left a roll of dark blue paper and a fluff of cotton wool fluttered over towards us and the cattle. A steer, more curious than his mates, sniffed at the white ball — the last of our cook. Another thirty bob short!

With John gone, Doug took over the cooking. He had never cooked before and vowed vehemently he would never cook again even if it meant starving. All the same, with help and advice from Archie, he made a fair job of it, turning out edible dampers from water-logged damper-holes.

# 19.

# A DROVER'S LIFE HAS PLEASURES

With the fresh horses we had from Koolburra and Kalinga and with grass starting to shoot under our horses' hoofs we were able to do the usual stages — eight miles each day. At Laura we were able to cut down to a single watch at night which meant that each man had only to watch for half the time he had put in on the double-watch. This was the practice except for a night of exceptionally heavy rain or when on a bad, boggy camp until the cattle were sold.

Our losses had mercifully dwindled to none but the diseases were still with us and there had been no rain where we were.

From Coen to Laura the drovers' road follows the monotonous straightness of the Telegraph Line that goes to the tip of Cape York. With its wide clearing kept free of undergrowth by the linesman it is possible to see miles ahead and while we were travelling short stages we could sometimes see in a glance our route ahead for the next two days.

Along the Line are ant-beds, tall, angular, magnetic anthills lined up in formation and pointing more or less the same way. As we came closer to Fairview telegraph station and Laura a few welcome bends altered the straightness of the Line as we came into hills and basalt — the outside fringe of the country where ants paint the tree-trunks in bright reds, yellows and greys, depending on the colour of the earth from which they make their tunnel-tracery on the bark. It is rather a strange sight to see a forest of trees painted for twenty to thirty feet of their straight, slim height in warm earth colours. At first glance it is difficult to credit the small ants with the success of such an overwhelming painting project.

We had just left behind the last of the Fairview gates when a rider caught us up with a telegram for me. Nancy was well again but Dawn's little girl was now ill. Could I come for Nancy?

It was a relief to know for sure what was happening and that Nancy had recovered even though young Sherrill had now succumbed to the fever. Catching a fresh horse at the camp I rode into Laura where I tried unsuccessfully again to get in touch with Dawn and arrived back at the camp at midnight — in time to intercept, in the murky darkness, a cow heading back to her dead calf.

Bill was due to dip at Laura and was not relishing the thought of having only four hands to take the cattle through the very rough, broken country between Laura and the Block Fence. There were still closer to eleven hundred than to a thousand. He wanted me to arrange for Nancy to come down on the rail-motor from Cooktown the next day and to carry her as I had often done before while I kept my tailers on the move.

The lady whom I rang to pass the message on to Dawn said emphatically that this was an impossibility and that I should be ashamed of myself for leaving the children to go joy-riding around the countryside! The best thing I could do was to come to Cooktown on the motor myself.

Dawn wasn't consulted but there wasn't much I could do. I knew, of course, what I had to do, but I also saw Bill's point of view. This did not make the decision any easier. He had started off with "crook" cattle, not enough men to handle them and a dry route but now he was even more short-handed with John and me gone and the roughest country to traverse ahead of him.

I went down on the motor. Bill dipped. The Wet came in with a wallop. All this happened in one day.

The Laura-Cooktown railway line had a "new" rail-motor. That meant a second-hand one cast off by some more up-to-date line but of a slightly later vintage than the old "Leaping Lena" had been. It had made a recent triumphal entry into Cooktown perched precariously on the back of a semi-trailer, complete with a passenger travelling up the Mulligan Highway from Cairns in a rail-motor — by courtesy of the truckie.

The old motor certainly was due for retirement. I wore riding clothes, boots, leggings, a ten-gallon hat and a raincoat and I rode inside the rail-motor. Long before I reached Cooktown I was soaked through with rain. The roof leaked and the only glass in the windows seemed to be the windscreen in front of the driver.

One of my travelling companions was a drover who had heard we were short handed and came out to meet us at Fairview. He looked the mob over before he asked for a job and must have found it wanting. In any case he left without asking and told me and my travelling companions that it was the worst mob of cripples he'd seen and that we'd never get them to Mareeba.

Arriving in Cooktown I was very pleased to see that Sherrill was almost over her illness and that Nancy was totally recovered though Dawn looked as if she might be the next on the sick list. Not wanting to be stranded in Cooktown for the Wet I lost no time in finding a way home again. Abbie Lee, a very good friend to have in times of trouble, offered to take me out in his truck if I could be ready to leave in an hour. I could and we left. We beat the rain to Harvest Home but Abbie was bogged on his way home.

With the monsoonal rain soaking down continuously day and night, it felt good to be back with old Arthur. Who but a fool would hanker for leaky tents and jangling horse-bells when one had a comparatively dry roof overhead! But when Stan came past the door with three hundred head of fat cattle bound for the same sale as Bill's, with no "Sickness", no calves and only an odd one lame or blind, I felt a little heart-sick for my cripples on the tail.

Stan had hardly left (wearing my fleecy lined coat and still shivering) when I sat down to answer the many frantic letters from my mother that awaited my return. I had just written, "I don't know how Bill is getting on now," and had paused to chew the end of the pen and to stare into the rain and cogitate when, through the grey of a passing shower, a horseman appeared. It was Paddy from Butcher Hill. He had a note.

Roughly paraphrased it read, "Joyce will mind Nancy at Butcher Hill. (Joyce was flooded-out each Wet from Laura Station) Short-handed. Blight and foot-rot bad. Swam the river five times between Laura and the Block. Leaving Molly and your saddle at Maitland. Hurry." The signature — "your loving mate."

Once again wet clothes were wrapped in plastic and clothes being boiled-up on the stove were added to them in their hot steamy state. As Paddy and I had only two horses between us for Nancy's clothes, my swag and the three of us, I had to leave behind the "town" clothes, shoes etc I had so carefully carried to Coen and back to wear in Mareeba. Two shirts, two pairs of riding trousers, a towel and toilet gear were hastily stowed in a small swag. The wet clothes went into a sugar-bag hung over Paddy's mare's wither to balance the mailbag. Paddy took the swag. I took Nancy.

We said "Goodbye" to Arthur who took it all in his stride. We were gone within a half-hour of Paddy's arrival for, as he said, the rivers were rising.

The rivers were high — but not bad. This time we were able to walk and lead our horses over the "big" Normanby bridge, as, with water swirling within a couple of feet of the rough decking, it was too big a swim for the horses.

While I was eagerly waiting to see young John, he could not have cared less. He had his two cousins to play with, plenty of company and attention — so what was one old mother more or less!

Paddy caught and saddled a fresh horse for me and I left for Maitland without delay, keen now to see Bill and my poor tailers again. I reached the foot of the Byerstown Range in time to go up with Stan and his cattle. Though Stan had only a small mob, the range road was very steep and narrow. The cattle had to be taken up in "cuts".

A man went in the lead of the cattle. Behind him alternated a small "cut" of cattle and then another drover and another "cut" until all the cattle were accounted for and Stan, as the last man, brought up the tail. In this way, if a beast in any of the small mobs strayed from the literally "crooked and narrow" to go up or down either side, the drover had only to ride a comparatively short distance to get around the animal and put it back in the mob.

As the range road was excessively stony, it was absolutely imperative to keep the cattle stringing along steadily in the right direction to guard against unnecessary lameness.

At Maitland, Bill had left instructions. I was to leave the Butcher Hill horse there. Molly and my own saddle and bridle were waiting for me. Bill was to camp on the top side of the Palmer River.

"Where's Miles?" a stupid question, for even I should have been able to track the remaining nine hundred through the bog.

Miles went all coy and all he would say was that I couldn't miss it and that it was the big gully this side of the Palmer. I had a fleeting thought of riding on to the Palmer and then coming back one gully. In the background Miles's mate Ian was spluttering.

Finally, to Miles's acute embarrassment and Ian's amusement, I found out that the camp would be at Bastard Gully. The name had been changed from Cartwheel Gully by an exasperated drover many years ago. It lived up to its name. It was steel and narrow and paved, the wrong way round, with slate that was placed vertically rather than horizontally so that it was almost impossible to coax cattle across it.

The original name had been taken from a heavy cartwheel that had been abandoned there after it had been used to "grade" the surface of the old wagon road.

Along with "Bog-a-Duck" and "Dead Finish", Bastard Gully

made a refreshing change from the assortment of from One- to Twenty Four-mile Creeks which dotted the road.

At Spear Creek, Doug and Archie were boating the packsaddles and loads across in a berkmyre "boat" — a rectangle of berkmyre tarpaulin (our tucker tent, actually) secured at either end with straps to resemble a cross between a badly made canoe and an empty pea-pod. The gear was stowed methodically with packsaddles on the bottom to make the "ribs" of the vessel and more straps were tied about the gaping middle. Thus trussed it was propelled by swimming manpower across the swollen stream. These "boats" are unbelievably buoyant but clumsy and a bit hard to control in eddies and currents.

Miles had thoughtfully sent Black Norman with me in case the creek was a swim. Johnnie Douglas had been drowned there years ago to the consternation of the old hands. "Fancy getting himself drowned in Spear Creek!"

I did not wish to repeat his performance and to add my grave to his on the rocky outcrop at Harvest Home. Norman gallantly rode across with me but we didn't even have to remove our saddles to cross.

I met Bill and the cattle on dinner-camp. It was quite a happy picture despite the drizzle. The cattle, lessened by a hundred and sixty heifers cut out at Butcher Hill were full and content. We had hoped the Boss would have taken out the ones in the mob that were unable to travel easily but that wasn't to be. In any case, some of my old mates were now feeding about and one or two were even lying down chewing their cuds. Grass there was in abundance — water in super-abundance.

The Three Day Sickness, thought to be spread by a high-flying midge, disappeared with the rain but reappeared once again when the sun came out. With the mob down to just under nine hundred head and the route in good order things were looking up. The intensely stony road was the only drawback especially as the sand north of Laura had abraded the hoofs and the rain had subsequently softened them. Rock and stone had to be avoided at all cost.

There were quite a few lame ones despite our precautions. A few more dropped back onto the tail each day so Bill decided to shoe — or correctly to "cue" — them. He caught the first literally napping on dinner-camp and had him securely held with greenhide ropes before he woke up. That was easy.

The hard part was to nail the cues — old, worn, broken halves of cast-off horse-shoes to a cloven "toe". The bovine hoof has a very fine wall and is usually very hard. To drive the smallest size racing-plate into this paper-thin wall was made more difficult by the "give" in the beast's leg. It couldn't be held like a horse's hoof for shoeing for obvious reasons.

Some of the hoofs were infected and a hammer tap could bring a purulent spurt from a burst pocket of infection. Bill overdid his first job of cue-ing on Broken Bull. He put a half shoe on each toe of the four hoofs. The usual is to cue the outer toes only.

It was comical to watch the first old stag in his new shoes. As soon as he'd tentatively touch a shod toe to the ground, he would swiftly pull it up again making it difficult for him to retain his balance. He soon became used to them and set off purposely to make his way up amongst the tailers from his position of absolute last to one five or six places further forward.

Before we reached the saleyards, Broken Bull had many mates in new shoes. Before cue-ing they had been so tender they could barely stand but with their shod hoofs they were all able to feed along with the mob.

Stan, with his small mob of fresh cattle, soon caught up with us, camping within sight each night and then passing us about a week from Mareeba in order to dip first at the strategic cattle-dip at Font Hill.

Another mob of eight hundred from just this side of Coen also caught up but kept a respectful distance a day behind us. They were all company though and we sometimes met a drover from either mob in the course of a day's work.

Strangely, neither of these other two mobs had any Three Day Sickness.

With the rest of the mob feeling so well that they now bucked and played as they were counted off each day in the first light, the lame and the halt on the tail were sadly out-paced. They came along in a small select mob of their own so that Bill made it official and left me with about sixty of the worst hospital cases and I kept them going steadily, reaching camp well after the others had settled for the night.

In this way, the cripples were neither hustled nor bustled and almost all reached Mareeba. When darkness fell we stopped where we were, the old stags usually lying down where I left them. There we waited until Bill, having put the main mob on camp, came back to help me take them along in the dark.

If there was to be a moon, I waited for it and then travelled on to camp in the moonlight. By necessity we travelled at less than snail pace — but we got there. I had a rather affectionate admiration for the way these old stags and pikers battled on and it was a rather disconcerting thought to think of my old mates, Broken Bull among them, ending up as Camp Pie or Blood and Bone.

We were only one and a half days out from Mareeba when we were almost caught in a flash flood. There had been only a misty drizzle where we were but further upstream must have suffered a phenomenal cloud-burst.

Arriving slowly at the tiny creek near the camp, we were about to feed the cattle onto the night camp when the tiny creek turned into an ocean, complete with waves and foam. Water came down in waves as we tried to push the anxious cattle across but before we could do so, the creek broke its banks and spread out in a growing back-water behind us. With water on three sides and us with our whips and loud shouts on the fourth, the cattle had little alternative but to step into the raging torrent and once they took that first step that took the ground from under their feet, the waters assumed control.

They were whisked downstream and deposited on the other bank at a bend below the camp. All but one reached the other side but it was well after 8 p.m. before the crossing was accomplished.

It was very dark. The water was barely visible as a murky, greyish mass with black tree-tops dotted through it and white snatches of current eddying and swirling. This was definitely not inviting.

Thinking the boys intended to strip and swim across, I let them go first but they swam fully clothed and were gone before I realised I could have joined them. They were all strong swimmers and left their horses hobbled-out with the lone steer, preferring to swim across by themselves.

My choice was to go with my horse, slipping off on the upstream side and gripping the mane and reins as the horse began to swim but Molly would not swim. Bill swam over and returned with my big brown horse Garnet. He was a champion swimmer as big as the mountain he was named for and with a heart to match. He had already carried me over the Palmer, a branch of the Mitchell and several small creeks. He was one of the horses we used to carry things that we didn't want to get wet.

As I sat astride Garnet bareback, quite confidently, with the water lapping at his knees Bill gave me a little pep talk.

"Watch our for trees. If old Garnet hits one, jump clear of him or you'll get kicked. Keep his head up-stream. There's a bad limb there" he broke off to indicate with a hand-sweep a blur of rough water mid-stream — "Watch out. If you come off, get away from him quick and grab a tree if you don't think you can make it to the bank."

Very encouraging! The pep-talk must have affected Garnet, too, as three times I urged him into the water and each time he reared straight back and swung around as soon as he lost his footing.

"I'll stop here," I decided, not one to push my luck too far. "You've got to come back for the steer and the horses. I'll camp this side and come over in the daylight."

I was quite happy with my decision and though Bill considered me lacking in brain-power to prefer to sleep supper-less and swag-less in the drizzle, he left me to it.

On the way back, Bill and the still-unwilling Garnet parted

company as Garnet hit a submerged tree. Bill cut his chest from side to side but both reached the camp safely if separately.

My first intentions were to light a fire for my private use but after picking up something that seemed to wriggle I let the tiny blaze die out for lack of fuel. I expect snakes had just as much right to the one bit of high ground as I had so I curled up on my plastic saddle-cover, put my raincoat (also plastic) over me and went to sleep.

Twice I woke when the underside of the raincoat was wet, presumably from condensation and the third time I woke when Bill came over at 2 a.m. after his watch to take me back. We rode back together through water knee-deep! It had run down as swiftly as it had flooded.

# 20.

# AFTER THE SALE IS OVER

The sale could hardly be referred to as a success. We counted eight hundred and sixty-seven head into the yards with an agent counter-checking and were paid for eight hundred and fifty-eight. Where the eight disappeared from the yards no-one could tell us.

The other non-paying passenger was one of my mob, old Broken Bull with his fancily shod feet. Happy Mac, the meatworks buyer refused to pay for him as he said he wouldn't make the forty-six miles by rail to the meatworks in Cairns. I suggested he leave him and we'd shoot the poor old fellow then and there.

"Aw, don't be so tough!" was Mac's comment and Broken Bull was loaded on. And I'll bet that trip was child's play after the one he'd done. But it was a case of no "sale" no droving money so we were another thirty bob down.

The small low-level crossing between the saleyards and the town flooded during the sale and one by one buyer's vehicles pulled out as their owners' left for the "safe" side of Granite Creek.

A large pen of eighty cows, many of them being the ones that had calved the dead calves and which I had nursed back to health were sold for £3/2/6 ($6.25) a head. The mob also included all the speyed cows. As a by-stander remarked, "Put a bit more to it and you can buy a turkey!"

With £2 ($4) to go to Fred for mustering and £1/10/- ($3) to us for droving, Hardy didn't make a fortune out of that pen.

The boys left us at Mareeba after the sale and returned home by 'plane from Cairns. Bill and I brought the plant back together with a small mob of mares and foals we had bought to augment our future horse supply. All told, we left with over fifty head that plunged in fifty different directions in the bog with the bought mares, their baby foals and their yearlings, all totally unused to bog, whinnying shrilly and piling up upon each other in their panic.

Fortunately, not all the horses belonged to us and some were to be left at Font Hill for another drover.

We reached Font Hill just a few minutes ahead of the floods but there was no one at home. We waited too long for them to return — we had left a mare behind in a paddock on our way to Mareeba — and the floodwaters beat us.

The river rose higher and higher. At first Bill cantered down to the crossing every few hours in the vain hope that the waters might subside. With the enormous volume of water coming down he soon gave up all hopes of getting out. We put up a tent, made camp and prepared to make the best of it.

On the opposite side of the river, but with Molloy township as their base, our absent hosts were likewise stranded.

We had plenty of company though, for, when sale dates have been set, drovers and their charges must go through hell and high-water to reach their destination.

As all the cattle, roughly two thousand head, in the three mobs travelling for our sale had played up in the long lane leading to the Font Hill yards, I wanted to see how the turmoil appeared from a spectator's point of view. As a participant it was rather frightening.

Ours rushed back twice, once before my band of cripples had arrived within the lane and once after we had. Being with eighteen hundred, give or take a few, thrusting, rattling and knocking horns and almost three and a half thousand trampling feet in a small railed enclosure — with the hoofs and horns gaining rapidly as the horsemen try vainly to turn them back — is a discomforting experience. However, I thought it would be well worth watching — at a safe distance of a hundred yards or so with a low branching tree handy if possible.

I was to be disappointed. Mob after mob strung in, like milkers' calves, to be dipped.

The first mob through was a small one, just under four hundred head and over seventy of these came from another drover's mob. The Mitchell River had been a big swim. The drover had managed only to get the first seventy-odd of his mob across when the leaders began to ring, circling around and around in the brown water, water-sleek red backs dipping and bobbing in the current and horns knocking and interlocking. Cattle are excellent swimmers but this mob, despite all efforts of the drovers, finally came out onto the bank they had originally left and refused to try again.

Perhaps they could hardly be blamed for that as they came from alligator country and were unusually wary of watercourses. Thwarted at the Mitchell, the drovers followed another mob along an alternate route through the tiny settlements of Carbine and Molloy exchanging the terrors of the Mitchell for mile after mile of belly-deep bog.

Norman, with his elder brother George, had George's cattle and the seventy-odd swimmers. George who usually looked more than a little like a kangaroo dog in full training, looked even more hollow and boney. He had good reason. He had been bitten by a red-back, the small harmless-looking black spider with the drop of bright crimson on his back. Legs and all, they could easily fit on a threepenny bit but they pack a power of poison in their small package.

As they, too, were short-handed, George had to endure the burning fever and the shivering fits, suffer the weakening nausea and the headaches, put up with the pain that suffused his whole body — and keep riding. Cattle — if not their keepers — have to be looked after day and night.

Norman had his worries as well though they were trivial compared to his brother's. A scorpion, angered at finding an intruder in the beautiful rain-proof shelter he had just discovered, fastened his burning pincers into Norman's scalp as he went to put his hat on in the half-light.

I found a great, five inch long yellow centipede in the sweat-band of my hat but being warned by the rattle and scratch of his hundred legs as he approached my ear-hole, I removed him in time, though perhaps with a remarkable lack of dignity and restraint.

To even things up, Bill found a snake in the pocket of his swag and with Norman, at a safe distance, holding the carbide light, quickly despatched him. The snake was a pretty little fellow, pencil-slim and short, his body painted in alternate bands of black and white. Up here they are called "ring snakes" and have the reputation of being able to inflict a very nasty bite.

Ruth's Fred was the next through with his mob. They were similar in shape and size to ours except that he lacked the calving cows. He also had no Three Day Sickness. The bog in the yards by this time was so deep that one of the smallest steers, knocked over by a larger cousin, fell head-down and smothered in the few seconds it took to reach him. To be driven three hundred miles from home only to be drowned in mud!

With the third mob that passed while we were stranded, our natural history knowledge was extended. We were sitting around a carbide light — the boys had the fire — in company with assorted sizes of cane toads. The toads are certainly ugly, for repulsive looks few can eclipse them, but they have their uses. Where toads have infiltrated the snake population has decreased. The unsuspecting frog-eating snake takes himself a poisoned bait when he samples toad.

Among the toads present were some babies about the size of a two shilliing piece — sorry, twenty cents!

"They reckon," began Rod, prodding a small one into position with a twig and guiding him towards his big brother, "that the big ones eat the little ones."

Hardly had he begun to speak but the larger toad swung around, leapt six or seven inches and in the one movement, engulfed the little bloke. We were speechless. We were amazed. We also were convinced.

Our absent hosts returned in time to help dip Rod's cattle, They were custodians for the Government-maintained dip and had to count all cattle passing through it. The drovers obligingly left their cattle numbers in their forced absence.

The McDowells also decided they would help us across the river as they had just swum across.

Horses are easily drowned if they are washed against a tree and foals are double trouble. I didn't think I would have been much help to Bill if we had struck a mid-stream pile-up so we were very grateful for their offer. We went to look at the river. It was still very high but there was the possibility it could rise still higher so a course of action was planned.

Later that evening the men were to swim the pack-horses across, taking the gear over by "boat" and continuing until a second stream was crossed. The horses were then hobbled, bell-tongues loosed and the packs elevated on fallen limbs and securely covered.

Next morning, all we had to do was to get ourselves, the saddle-horses and the mares and foals across. I crossed first — on the downstream handle of a galvanised iron wash-tub! Jim was on the top-side handle and in the tub were my clothes, saddle, bridle and our swag. Jim's wife had left her swim-suit hanging in a high tree for such emergencies and I appreciated being able to swim in it rather than dragging across in heavy, wet riding gear.

Though Nancy was my size, the men — six feet tall and built to match — had obviously borrowed the suit before and it no longer clung to its feminine shape. With only a piece of rotten string knotted around the slack the proprieties were barely observed.

The tub was the recognised form of wet-weather transport across the river. It made an excellent boat but I didn't fancy taking small children over in it as Nancy and Jim did whenever they needed to cross.

"How do the little boys like it?" I asked.

"Oh, the little bloke likes it all right but the biggest fellow keeps trying to jump out," was the reply.

Once over and dressed, I saddled my horse and waited ready to shepherd the other horses together as they emerged from their swim. What a time it took! To ensure that the horses did not overcrowd, they were sent over in small batches. The mares and foals were left until last hoping the presence of their mates on the other bank would encourage them to swim straight over.

It was good to watch the men in the water. They were absolutely fearless and would swim into a muddle of threshing horses and flailing steel-shod hoofs, sort the animals out and with a loud hand-slap and a splash of water, set them on their correct route once more. Jim hurt his ankle when five horses, all struggling together, pushed his leg against a tree. The bottom horse of the five was almost drowned by the time Boof and Bill, helped by Jim as soon as he was free, separated them and steered them, one by one, to the bank.

The foals were a bit difficult. They would reach the bank, then, instead of following their mothers up the other side, would wheel and swim back whinnying shrilly all the way. Of course the mares then wanted to go back to them! The foals were eventually crossed by the men taking the foals, one to a man. They swam beside them, often with an arm across the foal's neck and prevented them from going the wrong way by well-placed slaps and splashes.

The second creek was neither as wide nor as strong as the first but the horses had seen enough water for the day and were reluctant to go bathing again so soon. Brute force, bad language, much galloping and associated yelling finally prevailed and after our friends helped us to re-pack they left us and we were again on our own with our horses' heads pointed for home.

# 21.

# I BUILD MY OWN CHAIN

If I had thought I was through with driving cripples I was mistaken. The stony road played up even worse with the soft Tableland-bred hoofs than with the tough, old road-cattle. It was impossible to shoe the foals and the yearlings and to shoe the mares would have meant unnecessary misery for the others as the shod mares would walk out more briskly and travel too fast for the foals.

Bill went ahead with the plant-horses when necessary to get to camp to do some chore and I tagged along with the lame ones.

Going down the Byerstown Range was particularly painful to all. There were about three miles of winding road in the climb down and it took us three and a half hours to make the descent. Thank heavens it was the last stage to Butcher Hill. We were almost home.

It was March. None-the-less it was still good to open the huge stack of Christmas mail that had accumulated with the later fortnightly offerings. The lateness detracted none from the usual excitement of getting parcels in the bush. Watched by the children, I opened my gifts and distributed the greeting cards equally between them. We had been on the road for three months.

That was the end of my brief droving career but for Bill it was just the beginning. With the new and growing cattle herd below the Block Fence and trips each year during the droving season as well as helping-out at Butcher Hill, Bill was home even less than before.

Once back at Harvest Home, Arthur and I settled into a very comfortable existence. We accumulated a decent milking herd, grew a few vegetables and planted fruit trees, tried our hand rather successfully (I did the trying and Arthur the advising) at drying slices of pumpkin, sweet potato and banana for the drovers as well as making hobble straps and repairing the gear.

I counterlined saddles under Jock and Gladys' strict instruction and generally saw that the gear was always in good order and ready for the next trip.

The two Tableland poddies were no trouble to milk but the other two cows weren't as co-operative. They were Zebu/black poll crosses descended from the Robbins bull who came to Mowbray near Port Douglas at the turn of the century from the Melbourne Zoo. They had a certain independence of spirit which is anything but an asset in a milking cow.

For the first year I was forever in difficulties with kicked-over milk buckets (always when nearly full and never when almost empty!) and kicked shins. Both black Zebu cows were uncowed and athletic. Jock was no comforter. He told me how lucky I was as the black polls at Starcke were said to bite. Arthur suggested I turn the black cows back out "bush" but I persevered knowing the ignominy that would result if I "spoilt" Bill's "good, quiet cows".

The next year when they came back in to milk they equalled the Tablelanders in behaviour and surpassed them in milk-production so the training period (of self and cow) was worth it.

As the droving trips continued, almost always "in the Wet", the pack-bags deteriorated well beyond the stage where they could be patched or laced-up so I decided to try my hand at tanning greenhide and making Bill another set to surprise him when he came home.

Jock tanned side after side of beautiful pliable leather and gave me his recipe. Unfortunately he was busy and neither he nor Gladys could supervise.

First of all, the hide had to be de-haired by leaving in a lime bath. I think this is where I made my first mistake. The corrugated appearance and ironlike hardness of my "leather" seemed to indicate I'd overdone the treatment and "burnt" it but the great difficulty I had in scraping any hair off gave the lie to this theory.

After de-hairing it had to be soaked in a mixture of which the main ingredient was the white portion of fowl manure. Jock said this contained the necessary chemical to make the hide ready to accept the tan. The tan itself was concocted from Ironwood bark, freshly gathered from a tree whose bark was "not too brown, not cocoa-ish but a good juicy red". With my tomahawk I tried all the trees within a two mile radius of the house and found their bark was almost always in the black to cocoa category.

The one furtherest from the house had the least offensive shade of cocoa so I settled for that and cut a sugar-bag of bark to take home. There it was pounded to break the fibre and stewed in the copper clothes-boiler for a day.

When the tan had cooled I slipped the prepared hide into its strained waters with a silent prayer to the Patron Saint of Tanners. He wasn't listening and it was then that poor Aboriginal Hilda suffered her stroke and was paralysed down one side. The intricate and important timing was upset but I kept on and gathered the second and then third lots of bark from the same tree.

Strangely, I was still optimistic and though the "leather" looked terribly hard and unyielding I thought working it over a rail to "break" it and then treating it with an application of fat might make it pliable.

I was still working on it when Jock and Gladys rode up almost unnoticed.

"Cripes!" exclaimed Jock after a swift but critical examination of my work. "Setting up a corrugated iron factory?"

As we were drinking the inevitable tea he confided,

"If I were you, I wouldn't leave it around where people can see it."

It finally found its niche as a quite waterproof roof for a chicken coop and when Jock and Gladys next rode over each carried a roll of beautifully tanned leather. Bill got his new pack-bags.

At Merluna, Iris was in more strife. After Beth's birth at the station Iris decided they needed an airstrip for emergencies and she and the gins were clearing light timber from what was later to become their landing-strip.

In the process, Iris received a snake bite on the arm. She immediately ligatured it with a tie from Beth's sunbonnet and cut the wound (herself!) with a razor-blade as soon as young Mike and Peter broke all records getting back with one from the house.

It was due to a fair amount of good luck as well as her quick thinking and good management that Iris was able to see the sun rise the following day. Rapidly becoming nauseated and generally "ill" she hastily instructed the native women how to make-up Beth's bottles. They retreated with her to their camp, there to wail all night and to rock Beth to sleep with a charming little improvised lullaby that went "Poor little Bubba. 'e got no Mumma. What we do with poor little Bubba?"

Bill broke his leg while mustering with a friend and had to ride the best part of twenty miles to the station before he could get transport to Cooktown. Much to Matron's disgust — she was omniscient, nothing ever escaped her knowledge — his plaster didn't stop him from riding.

He would hobble out on his crutches to catch the little night-mare and although it took a while for her to get used to him with his four legs, he would ride off with the spare legs over his shoulder to do his day's work. In spite of this, the leg healed well and he left to take delivery of his first mob of the season a week after his last plaster was removed.

Two days after Bill left home to bring the bullocks down I

The droving plant in the Stewart River.

The plant at the Hann 150 miles further south.

Connie Gostelow (nee Callaghan) at Laura Sports.

"Pluto" Sykes, a happy ringer (cowboy).

The mob searches for feed as it travels slowly down the Port Stewart Range on the long trek south.

Heralding the end of an era – the beginning of the end of the droving days and the start of motor road transport for cattle, 1959.

began to miscarry what would have been our third child. We had no vehicle, no radio and Jock and Gladys were camped out and thus not likely to call. Arthur was getting fidgety and put his old horse, Ronnie, in the night paddock with Little Old Fashioned Mare.

Providentially, a chance caller took me to town where I spent a few days before returning. Matron was at a conference. The trouble didn't end there and I had poor Arthur a nervous wreck before Jock and Gladys called in while mustering outside our paddocks.

Arthur didn't know whether to leave me and ride to Helenvale for help or to stay. Gladys had no such indecision. She didn't like what she saw so they rode home for the truck and rushed me off to town.

Once there and with Matron back in charge, she decided it would be better for me to hitch a ride to Atherton hospital with an obliging stock agent and a cattle-buyer than to wait till first light the next morning for an Aerial Ambulance.

In the weeks before I left for Atherton hospital, Arthur's main contribution to tea-time conversation was how he had just read in "Readers' Digest" that a woman could bleed to death in a matter of minutes. I worried him much more than rushing bullocks ever did in his forty years of droving!

Not long after I returned, Arthur became ill. He was an independent old chap and turned down the offer of a lift to Cooktown with Padre and Mrs Colin Ford, preferring to ride off alone on old Ronnie to Helenvale. By that time he was unable to protest too much. In any case Mrs Leary was strong-minded too. She sent an urgent call to Norman and sent Arthur to town in Norman's truck after ringing Matron.

Matron, in her turn, flew Arthur to Cairns almost immediately but it was too late. He didn't return. He was over eighty and had lived a good life by his own reckoning but, even so, it is sad to see the old hands go. He was a true pioneer of the Peninsula.

The family showed an increase that year all the same. Iris had another baby boy. Ruth presented young "Saltbush" with a brother and, despite the bad beginning, we kept up with them and Bill junior was born, like Iris' Harding, at Atherton. Cooktown, being in a doctor-less state, was out of bounds to freight-carrying storks and brolgas!

The time had also come when Johnnie, correspondence lessons and I became acquainted. The partnership thus formed was anything but a pleasurable one. Home-tutoring mothers will understand. No one else could possibly envisage the agony of it all.

In Coen, due to the tireless efforts of the Coen folk and the A.I.M. couple, Colin and Margaret Ford, the staff were already in residence, and in service, at the new cottage hospital. Also in residence were four young station children who were living there and receiving their education at the local school.

As the Coen hospital project had only been given the official go-ahead a short twelve months previously, it was little short of a miracle that this well-equipped, modern hospital was firmly planted on its own little rise overlooking the isolated out-post township. The people of the Peninsula had not quite become used to it nor could they totally believe their good fortune.

As well as the enormous material difference it was to make to their lives and their comfort, it also made the outside world take notice. All over Australia people were now becoming interested in our welfare. Weipa bauxite had caused a lot of excitement and speculation. People were looking at their maps of Queensland and were finding that, contrary to popular belief, Queensland extended way beyond Cairns — almost to New Guinea!

Progress was on its way. The peace of the Peninsula was about to be broken. Its resurrection day was not too far ahead.

# 22.

# QUINKEN

Annie, half-sister to Micky Blue-tongue the old yard-boy at Butcher Hill, was a child welfare expert. The Boss sent her down to stay with me after Arthur Jones died. I was expecting our third baby and Bill was mustering at Butcher Hill.

Each night by bed-time the children's hair was on end as a result of Annie's bed-time stories. Annie was an authority on Quinken and the children had heard so much about them that when they did go away with me to "get the new baby", they were ecstatic to see two of them walking side by side down the Esplanade.

I don't think the two nursing nuns in their long, white gowns and veils heard their delighted cries of "Look Mummy! Really truly Quinken!" Or if they did they gave no sign.

Annie had once seen Quinken gathering lily roots from a swamp near her old Battle Camp home — a mother, a father and a baby. They spoke to her and Annie answered, for it is manners never to speak until spoken to, especially with Quinken.

Each night Annie carried her swag over and slept on the floor beside my bed. The early part of the night was punctuated with Annie's queries.

"What that noise, Missus? You hearem that one? That one Quinken throwing stones." The latter part of the night was made difficult for sleeping by the crescendo of Annie's snores.

There was one sound for which I could not find an explanation. I'd made several suggestions such as toads hitting the galvanised iron walls as they jumped after insects but Annie knew better than that. It was "Quinken throwing stones".

One night as Annie was snoring and I was lying awake I found the answer. On moonlight nights large brown beetles flew around, the odd one crashing to the floor near our kerosene lamp. Outside, the moonlight on the roof dazzled them. They hit it and rolled down the corrugations of the iron onto the ground. So much for the stones Annie's Quinken threw. Though I produced the beetles and gave what I thought was a persuasive demonstration of the hit and roll action, I don't think Annie was convinced.

Baby-craft was Annie's best subject. She could not understand why white women gave their babies milk from bottles when there were so many green-ants about. To have an abundant milk-supply all that was needed was to have enough green-ants to make a soup to drink and a puree to be rubbed on the reluctant mammary tissue. In two days, there would be "plenty milk for baby". Annie cited examples of "old, old woman" who brought up orphan babies in this way.

In my turn, I was unconvinced. I didn't have to resort to the green-ant treatment so can't say whether it would work on other than "old, old woman".

To cure children of bed-wetting, Annie recommended that the child's urine be gathered on a shovel and burnt in the fire. As the urine evaporated, the bed-wetting would cease. For babies who are slow to walk, Annie recommended holding them over the flames of the fire every morning so that the flames nearly touched their toes. The baby will soon respond and "run all-about". I do not recommend this to nervous mothers.

Annie was a cheerful person and the two children found her an ideal companion who was never too busy or too tired to take them fishing or just to talk to them. They usually cooked the results of the fishing expeditions on a small fire near Annie's hut but I would often find, pushed to the back of the stove, a milk-tin billy of stewing turtle or eel.

Johnnie wasn't a good pupil when it came to learning Annie's "language" but Nancy picked up a little and she and Annie sometimes entertained us at night by singing and dancing. The sight of roley-poley Annie complete with pipe and her tiny partner clad in long flannelette nightie, chanting and stamping out the rhythms was really worth seeing but it was performed only when the others were away.

Annie had a great collection of tribal beliefs she was willing to share. Members of her tribe were not allowed to eat "sugar-bag", the honey of the sting-less native-bee, if it were found in antbeds. I have only seen sugar-bag in wood, trees, stumps and fence-posts but Annie assured me "one kind" was found in antbeds. Nor could they eat a certain kind of lily. If they did, misfortune, if not sickness or even death, would follow.

A hot-water spring on the drovers' road was particularly potent. I told Annie I had "bogey-ed" (bathed) in it. She was incredulous and named two native boys who had died because they had gone into the spring and offended the water spirit there by doing so. In fact, one of Annie's enemies stole her "ploomers" (bloomers) from the camp at Laura races with the intention of throwing them into the spring. Fortunately a cousin of Annie's aunt discovered the plot, recovered the "ploomers" and saved Annie from a horrible death by "ploomer" proxy!

By the time Annie left for Butcher Hill, neither child would venture outside the lamp's circle at night and decided that "cukka" was easier to say than "bad" and "minya" every bit as satisfactory as "beef". A snake was a strange mixture of both languages a "cukka bitey".

Annie was replaced by Paddy's second wife who was brought up on a mission. Nevertheless, she promptly ran away back to Paddy on the second day because she was frightened of the Quinken. She covered the sixteen miles of the horse-road to Butcher Hill on foot and found where the plant was camped in a matter of hours.

Bill then sent down one of his regular droving "boys", old

Frank Kerr who told me he was a "grown man" when the Boss was a "picaninny". He took his name from one of J.S. Love's managers for whom Frank had worked both at Butcher Hill and at Battle Camp. Frank loved Quinken. I knew of four graves at Harvest Home on the hill just behind the yards. Three of them had ornate headstones and were enclosed within a wrought-iron fence.

Frank told me there were two more, one behind his camp and one in the night-paddock. He had worked here once too and the grave in the night-paddock belonged to a relation of his. Often I'd wake in the night to hear Frank carrying on a two-way conversation with one or other of the Quinken. He supplied both sides of the dialogue of course — or so I hope!

This communication was not without its advantages. Bill and I arrived home one night at about midnight to be met by a highly delighted Frank at the slip-rails that were our front gate.

"Hey, Boss! Boss, look!" From his hand he produced the bottom half of a set of false teeth. From his mouth he removed the other plate.

"You remember I lose 'em one time, long time ago? I tell Johnnie Douglas the other night and 'e say 'Frank, you look down the paddock where you cut that sugar-bag.' And I go look and I find 'im alright."

Frank gave us another wave with both plates for good measure before escorting us to the house and stoking up the fire to make a cup of tea for us.

He had lost the teeth two years before after a droving trip and Johnnie Douglas (who drowned in Spear Creek trying to save his half-brother) was brought home in a dray for burial on Christmas Day 1917 — about forty years before. While Johnnie drowned, his half-brother came ashore safely downstream.

Some turkey chickens I had were another of Frank's worries. I kept them in a wire-netted enclosure but the mother would fly out and the poults, in an attempt to follow her, sometimes became trapped in the mesh. If found quickly and released they survived but I lost a few before I decided to let them out during the day and lock them up only at night.

Frank was left in charge and as he was chopping firewood down the paddock he left the poults locked up in case they strayed but each time we'd return he'd greet us, no matter what the hour, with a mournful, "Ah, Missus, another chicky bin break 'is collarbone!"

I suppose it wasn't as bad as the greeting of another caretaker to the returning owners: "Boss, Missus, that 'pridge' (fridge or refrigerator) 'e proper dead!" It smelt a bit that way!

He had pulled the kerosene tank out to see if the flame was still going and didn't put it back properly so that the flame heated the underside of the fridge instead of liberating the gas to cool it. It had been full of freshly killed meat when they left.

After Frank's short turn as caretaker he went back to the Mission to find that his daughter, carefully locked each night in the girls' dormitory, was to become a mother. Frank collected his spears and set off in search of the baby's father — who fled — and the Mission Superintendent, who stood his ground.

As the result of his rampage Frank was sent to town in disgrace. He was to be sent to a mission further south. Frank didn't mind going down as he'd been there once before when the missions were evacuated during the war. While down there he had acted in a "real picture", had been in an aeroplane and had seen Ned Kelly's cave; but it was too cold down there for an old man and several of his contemporaries had recently died there.

We contacted the Superintendent and went to see the police with the result that Frank was "signed-on" to us again providing we took him straight out of town. Frank again became caretaker and spent most of his time telling me what he was going to do to all the "good Christian peoples" at the Mission.

At night he sat by his small fire tempering two hardwood spears and discussing the situation with his Quinken friends. He told me he was going to get permission from the Department of Native Affairs to spear in the leg both the Superintendent and the "boy" concerned for their part in his daughter's dishonouring. In Frank's mind the D.N.A. had taken over the duties of the council of elders.

Once back at the Mission after Frank's grandson was born, all was forgiven and Frank retired from droving and caretaking to grow peanuts.

Next time Bill went droving, I had Cecil (Cecily) and Joe. They had come from the mission near Cairns and station life was foreign to them. They found the isolation and lack of company very hard to bear and were always wanting to go back to the mission. I would have been more than willing for them to go but I was sure that if I did send them back something would happen to me and there would be no-one "to go for help", so we all suffered.

Finally they did go when I knew Bill was on his way back with the plant. But not before they had eaten nearly all the tinned fruit, a great luxury, from the store cupboard. I managed to save some by keeping it in the drawer with my clothes but by the time I'd found the cause of my dwindling supply it was almost too late. It was impossible to lock the door as Harvest Home didn't possess any doors or locks.

By some means of communication Joe and Cecil would arrange to meet the Kings Plains couple from the same mission at the bridge, an old but usable log structure half-way between the two homesteads. Cecil provided the tinned stuff and the others provided the eggs from Gladys' egg supply. But it wasn't until later that Gladys, getting out her petrol iron to get clothes pressed for town, found the methylated spirits she used for pre-heating had all been replaced with water, three bottles of it. At least it explained the "sick" turns her employees had been taking.

Hilda replaced Cecily and Joe. She was Frank's wife, part Aboriginal, part Japanese and part white. The three races combined to make a quite unique person. Hilda had been brought up by the Misses Gibson at Kings Plains and shared their surname. She spoke excellent English with the most mellifluous speaking voice I have ever heard. It looked as if my luck was in but two days after the plant left for Mareeba, Hilda had a stroke which paralysed her completely on one side and which kept her in hospital for many months before she made a partial recovery.

I had no driver's licence. I had been on the main road for the first time on my own the day before Hilda became ill when we drove out to the mail-box to get the mail. We managed to get half-way to town safely with Hilda trying to hold the baby, Billy, in her good arm. I refused to try to cross a bridge of bare, untrimmed slippery logs in the rain. It spanned a particularly dangerous-looking, fast-running stream. There was no point in tempting Providence I reasoned, so I left the three children, all under five, with my patient and walked upstream to the Helenvale pub. There Mrs Leary phoned the ambulance in Cooktown.

I was consoled to see that the ambulance driver didn't fancy the greasy hill either. He and the bearer crossed on foot and carried Hilda back on a stretcher.

Once out of hospital Hilda came back out to me as Bill was away again but though she was a welcome companion her health was too greatly impaired for my comfort at least. I was possibly prejudiced by the experience of a friend further up the Peninsula who was summoned early one morning with a

"Missus, quick. Maggie sick."

"How sick?" asked my friend as she put a dressing gown on.

"Oh, little bit sick."

Poor Maggie was dead on the doorstep. She had a heart complaint — unknown to the Missus — and had dropped dead as she opened the door on her way in to light the kitchen fire.

# 23.

# THE AWAKENING

Progress came to the Peninsula in different guises. The cattle industry benefited from the ending of the wartime meat agreement with Britain and the American discovery that North Australian bulls and old cows provided just the flavoursome, lean "ground" meat their hamburgers needed.

Cleanskin bulls were no longer shot. They were worth money. Aged branded bulls were walked in the mobs to the meatworks and saleyards to be replaced with younger, better bulls often with a dash of "Zebu".

The alumina at Weipa brought an awareness of the fact that there was, indeed, more of Australia north of Cairns and the old drovers' route gradually became a road trafficable by four wheel drive vehicles in the drier half of the year.

And last, but not least, Colin and Margaret Ford made their appearance. With Colin dressed in workmanlike but spruce khakis and Margaret unruffled in cotton they didn't fit into the preconceived idea of what a "parson" should look like, especially as they came ready and prepared to camp out in their swags and to cook over an open fire when necessary.

It was almost beyond the memories of the oldest inhabitants to recall previous visits from ministers of religion but soon the Fords and the practical Christianity they represented became the benchmark by which men of religion were to be measured.

There was a spate of christenings at remote homesteads when the Fords first arrived. One mother of a growing family couldn't remember if the two elder children had been christened. They had been born in the bush.

"Do 'em again to make sure," she suggested, and Colin Ford complied.

Many of the families visited were not theoretically of the religious denomination the Fords represented but the men reasoned that, if the "others" couldn't leave town to "brand-up", Colin Ford was welcome to the "cleanskins". The cleanskins were growing in number and the Fords, with their knowledge of the rest of Australia, were concerned about the lack of basic facilities for education and for medical treatment.

After much research into the problem three sites for a cottage — hospital-hostel were considered — Cooktown, which had a school and a hospital, Laura which had neither, and Coen which had no hospital but which had a small school that children could attend if a hostel were provided.

The Peninsularites were asked to cast their vote and Coen won the popularity stakes to the joy of harrassed mothers and the satisfaction of Police Sergeant Vince Moylan and John Harris of Coen who presented Coen's case to advantage.

Coen was to be the future home of a U-shaped cottage hospital to be staffed by two nursing sisters, with one arm of the "U" as a dormitory wing to accommodate the children who could then attend the tiny one-teacher State School.

Almost seven years after the Fords came into the northern area of Australia, the hospital-hostel was officially opened in August 1958. Sister Paskins, who had served previously in Cooktown and Sister Joy Ramsay were already in residence and at work.

It was a great day, not only for Coen, but for all the Peninsula when the township proper was deserted (Torrens' pub closed for the occasion) and the local population and ten times as many visitors crossed the breakaway gully separating the Hostel from the town to watch the Reverend Fred Mackay as superintendent of the Australian Inland Mission arrive by helicopter like a modern day Santa to open and to bless the enterprise. In reality the Reverend Fred had overlanded to Coen two days earlier but the helicopter entrance was an omen of changes to come. Civilisation had marched right in with the nursing sisters and their radio.

After the short ceremony the company adjourned to afternoon-tea. Stiff-collared clergy, city visitors, stockmen in tight-legged trousers and high-heeled Williams' boots, a stock squad detective and a lady "adventurer" from overseas squatted companionably on their heels to discuss things in general and to exchange the year's accumulation of news.

The men in their high-heeled boots tip-toed awkwardly across the spotless polished floor hesitating to add the clump of their boots to the noisy background whir of conversation as they sought out the huge hostel teapot.

The women tried to jam a year's talking into one short afternoon despite forays to rescue wandering children and trips into the men's domain with yet more tea and refreshments. And all the time cameras clicked and TV cameramen pointed their apparatus at all and sundry. Coen was News.

Clicko, one of Colin Gostelow's droving boys and a great actor, delighted the crowd with an impromptu emu dance with a bobbing bustle of emu "tail-feathers" fashioned from a grey plastic raincoat tucked in appropriate folds in his belt. His mates quickly marked the rhythm for his dance with hand-claps and click-sticks gathered from the twigs on the ground beside them.

The races were to follow on the next day but not until a Holy Communion service was held in the newly-dedicated building nor until Colin Ford had baptised young Bill, in the same meeting room and on our way to the races.

How different it seemed, outwardly at least, from when John and Nancy were christened at Harvest Home with water from the tank in an oatmeal bowl and with old Arthur and Margaret Ford as witnesses. And with Johnnie racing outside at the crucial moment with a hither-to hidden crust for Bulldog! Only the Padre's wonderful sincerity and the simple beauty of the biblical words were the same. It seemed so much further apart in time than those two short years.

Returning our visit, the clergy turned-out in full force to the race-meeting. The little Sister, explaining her ignorance of the betting jargon, confided apologetically that it was the first race-meeting she had attended. At the end of the day she still wore a slightly bewildered look.

"The Coen" is much like any other bush meeting except that, as a good part of the track lies in a hollow, you see the horses only at the start and the finish. It is quite a remarkable arrangement but not recommended for hyperactive punters. After all, it is the finish that counts and all were vying for top honours that day.

From the logs that formed part of the seating in the "grandstand" came the hoarse croaks of the bookies. "Two to one, bar one," or "I'll TAKE five to one" as the mood took them.

They had a bad day. The favourites and the punters won. Mick's horse won the coveted A.I.M. Trophy and it could not have happened to a more delighted horse-trainer. Six o'clock the following evening saw Mick spotless in his ceremonial whites with a neat maroon tie, trying to fill in time (and keep sober) until the prizes were presented at nine. Bill had ridden Mailman for Mick and a TV camera recorded the victory for posterity and the folk Down South who clustered around their sets.

Johnnie left me to trail about in the shadow of his current hero — the grader-driver. Nancy was beside me chatting to her cousins and Billy, having escaped from the natural log corral near the bookies, was trying hard to poke out a younger cousin's eyes.

Crick, cri-ick, cr-i-i-ck went the Aerial Ambulance's chocolate wheel as it came to an indecisive stop.

"Twenty-one! That's mine!" gasped someone and jumped up amid congratulatory murmurs to collect her prize.

A group of station blacks chuckled their way past to view

their fancy for the last race of the program — the blackboys' race. From the bar came the mournful strains of "Pub with no Beer" sung by a circlet of staggering celebrants.

As a punter for several gentlemen otherwise engaged I was trying rather hopelessly to calculate how much cash I held for each one. Each calculation became more confused and complicated due mainly because Billy had almost accomplished his mission and had to be forcibly restrained. Apart from that I had a headache and my legs were aching, signs of approaching old age and a life of dissipation.

It was no use trying to catch Bill's eye to take Junior. Bill was with the other jockeys weighing-in for the last race of the program.

I returned to my settling-up but a TV man was rounding us up to stand at the rails for a picture. That accomplished I returned to the mental arithmetic sorting out wins, losses and final balances.

In the background someone was asking Nancy how old she was.

"Too old," came the reply in tones so like my own that it could not fail to be disconcerting.

The figures I had so far successfully segregated into their owners' accounts merged once more into kitty. My legs ached and my head ached and swam at the same time.

Hazily, I heard a voice.

"And you, Mrs Wallace," Nancy's acquaintance was politely inquiring, "where are you from?"

I tried to sort it out in my jumbled mind — Nanango, Goondiwindi, Tully, Roma, Injune, Kingaroy, Bundaberg, Cooktown and Sydney. Three years spent here, two spent there and eighteen months somewhere else. Why, it was over seven years since the Boss, Ruth and I had flown home from Cairns on that April Fools' Day morning! Almost twice as long as I had lived in any other place!

My unpretentious bosom swelled with pride and a queer sense of gratification. I turned to the lady visitor just as she was about to repeat her question, surprising her with my emphasis.

"From the Peninsula," I replied, "from the Peninsula."

THE END

**Bush girls of Cape York Peninsula, 1955 – Shirley Porter, Lennie Wallace (author of this book) and the late Ruth Wallace.**

Books by

**Lennie Wallace**

*Bow Waves in the Bull Dust*

*Bitten by the Bull Bug*

*Nomads of the 19th Century Queensland Goldfields*

*The Battlers of Butchers Hill*

*Cape York Peninsula*

*From Nanango to Cooktown*